THE PHILOSOPHY OF RESTORATIVE JUSTICE

Dr. Maxwell Shimba

Printed in the United States of America

TABLE OF CONTENTS

INTRODUCTION

Overview of Restorative Justice

Restorative justice is a paradigm shift in the approach to justice, moving away from traditional punitive systems towards one that emphasizes healing, accountability, and reconciliation. At its core, restorative justice seeks to repair the harm caused by criminal behavior through cooperative processes that include all stakeholders. This approach is rooted in ancient practices and has evolved over centuries, gaining renewed attention and implementation in contemporary societies worldwide.

Explanation of Restorative Justice

Restorative justice is an alternative to the conventional criminal justice system, which often focuses on punishment and retribution. Instead, restorative justice emphasizes the restoration of relationships, the rehabilitation of offenders, and the healing of victims. It involves direct or indirect communication between the victim and the offender, with the support of the community, to address the harm caused and to find mutually agreeable ways to make amends.

Key components of restorative justice include:

1. Inclusion of All Stakeholders: Restorative justice involves victims, offenders, and community members in the resolution process, ensuring that all voices are heard and respected.

2. Focus on Repairing Harm: The primary goal is to repair the harm caused by the offense, rather than simply punishing the offender.

3. Accountability: Offenders are encouraged to take responsibility for their actions and to understand the impact of their behavior on others.

4. Voluntary Participation: Participation in restorative justice processes is typically voluntary, fostering genuine engagement and commitment to the resolution.

5. Facilitated Dialogue: A neutral facilitator often guides the dialogue between the victim and the offender, ensuring a safe and constructive conversation.

Origins of Restorative Justice

The origins of restorative justice can be traced back to Indigenous practices and traditional justice systems around the world. Many indigenous cultures, including those in North America, Africa, and New Zealand, have long utilized restorative approaches to resolve conflicts and restore harmony within their communities.

In North America, Native American tribes practiced forms of restorative justice through community-based dispute resolution processes. These practices emphasized healing, community involvement, and the reintegration of offenders into society. Similarly, in Africa, traditional justice systems, such as the Gacaca courts in Rwanda, focused on reconciliation and community healing following the genocide.

In New Zealand, the Maori people have a rich history of using restorative justice principles, which have significantly influenced the country's modern justice system. The Family Group Conference, a cornerstone of New Zealand's restorative justice approach, originated from Maori practices and has been widely adopted in various contexts globally.

Importance of Restorative Justice

The importance of restorative justice lies in its potential to transform the justice system and society as a whole. Several key benefits highlight its significance:

1. Empowerment of Victims: Restorative justice provides victims with a voice and an active role in the justice process, helping them to heal and find closure.

2. Rehabilitation of Offenders: By focusing on accountability and making amends, restorative justice

promotes the rehabilitation and reintegration of offenders into society.

3. Strengthening Communities: Restorative justice fosters community involvement and support, leading to stronger, more resilient communities.

4. Reduction in Recidivism: Evidence suggests that restorative justice can reduce recidivism rates, as offenders are more likely to change their behavior when they understand the impact of their actions and take responsibility.

5. Holistic Approach: Restorative justice addresses the root causes of crime and seeks to repair relationships, leading to more comprehensive and sustainable solutions.

In recent decades, restorative justice has gained recognition and adoption in various sectors, including criminal justice, education, workplaces, and communities. Its principles are being integrated into legal systems, policies, and practices worldwide, reflecting a growing acknowledgment of its effectiveness and transformative potential.

Structure of the Book

This book is structured to provide a comprehensive exploration of restorative justice, its philosophical foundations, practical applications, and transformative potential. The chapters will delve into the historical context, theoretical frameworks, core principles, and real-world examples of restorative justice in action. Additionally, the book will address the benefits, challenges, and future prospects of restorative justice, offering a visionary look at how it can reshape justice systems and communities.

By the end of this book, readers will have a deep understanding of restorative justice, its importance, and its potential to create a more just and compassionate society. The journey through these pages will reveal the power of restorative practices to heal, transform, and build stronger, more connected communities.

Purpose of the Book

Restorative justice represents a transformative approach to addressing harm and conflict that emphasizes healing, accountability, and community involvement. This book is designed to explore the philosophical foundations, practical applications, and transformative potential of restorative justice in a comprehensive and accessible manner. Through this exploration, the book aims to provide readers with a deep understanding of how restorative justice can reshape the way we think about justice and conflict resolution.

Philosophical Foundations

At its core, restorative justice is rooted in a rich tapestry of philosophical traditions that emphasize the importance of relationships, community, and ethical responsibility. The philosophical underpinnings of restorative justice draw from various schools of thought, including:

1. Relational Ethics: This perspective emphasizes the interconnectedness of individuals within a community and the ethical responsibilities that arise from these relationships. Restorative justice is grounded in the belief that harm impacts not just the individuals directly involved but also the broader community.

2. Communitarianism: Communitarian philosophy highlights the importance of community values and collective well-being. Restorative justice aligns with this by prioritizing the restoration of community harmony and the reintegration of offenders as productive members of society.

3. Virtue Ethics: Rooted in Aristotelian philosophy, virtue ethics focuses on the development of moral character and virtues such as empathy, compassion, and responsibility. Restorative justice practices encourage the cultivation of these virtues in both victims and offenders.

4. Restorative Ontology: This approach to understanding being and existence underscores the fundamental need for restoration and healing in the aftermath of harm. It posits that true justice can only be achieved when relationships are mended and communities are strengthened.

Practical Applications

The practical applications of restorative justice are diverse and extend across various contexts, including criminal justice, education, workplaces, and communities. This book will examine how restorative justice principles can be effectively implemented in these areas to address harm, resolve conflicts, and promote healing.

1. Criminal Justice System: Restorative justice offers an alternative to traditional punitive measures by focusing on rehabilitation and reconciliation. Case studies and examples will illustrate how restorative practices can reduce recidivism, support victim healing, and create safer communities.

2. Educational Settings: In schools, restorative justice can transform disciplinary approaches by fostering a supportive and inclusive environment. This book will explore successful implementations of restorative practices in schools and their impact on student behavior and academic achievement.

3. Workplace Conflict Resolution: Restorative justice principles can be applied to resolve workplace conflicts, improve employee relationships, and create a positive organizational culture. Practical strategies and examples will demonstrate how businesses can benefit from restorative approaches.

4.   Community   Programs: Community-based restorative justice programs can address various forms of harm, from minor disputes to serious offenses. The book will highlight innovative community initiatives and their role in building stronger, more cohesive communities.

Transformative Potential

The transformative potential of restorative justice lies in its ability to fundamentally alter the way we approach justice and conflict resolution. By focusing on healing, accountability, and community involvement, restorative justice has the power to create lasting positive change in individuals, relationships, and societies.

1. Empowerment of Victims: Restorative justice empowers victims by giving them a voice in the justice process and addressing their needs for healing and closure. This book will discuss the profound impact of victim-centered approaches on individual recovery and community trust.

2. Rehabilitation of Offenders: By encouraging offenders to take responsibility for their actions and actively participate in making amends, restorative justice promotes genuine rehabilitation and reintegration into society. Examples will illustrate how this approach reduces recidivism and fosters personal growth.

3. Strengthening Communities: Restorative justice fosters a sense of collective responsibility and community solidarity. The book will explore how restorative practices can build stronger, more resilient communities capable of addressing harm and preventing future conflicts.

4. Cultural and Systemic Change: The principles of restorative justice challenge existing power dynamics and promote more equitable and inclusive systems. This book will examine how restorative justice can drive cultural and systemic change, leading to more just and compassionate societies.

Structure of the Book

To achieve its purpose, this book is organized into several chapters, each focusing on different aspects of restorative justice:

1. Historical Foundations of Restorative Justice: Tracing the origins and evolution of restorative practices across cultures and time periods.

2. Theoretical Frameworks: Exploring the philosophical and ethical foundations of restorative justice.

3. Core Principles and Values: Delving into the key principles that underpin restorative justice, such as accountability, reparation, and community involvement.

4. Restorative Practices and Models: Examining various restorative justice practices and models, including victim-offender mediation, family group conferencing, and circle processes.

5. Case Studies and Real-World Applications: Highlighting successful implementations of restorative justice in different contexts.

6. Benefits and Challenges: Discussing the positive outcomes and common challenges associated with restorative justice.

7. Restorative Justice and the Legal System: Exploring the integration of restorative justice within traditional legal frameworks.

8. Restorative Justice in International Contexts: Providing a global perspective on restorative practices and their impact.

9. Restorative Justice and Social Justice: Examining the intersection of restorative justice with issues of race, gender, and social equity.

10. The Future of Restorative Justice: Speculating on the future directions and innovations in restorative justice.

Final Thoughts

Through a detailed exploration of the philosophical foundations, practical applications, and transformative potential of restorative justice, this book aims to provide readers with a comprehensive understanding of this powerful approach to justice and conflict resolution. By highlighting the importance of healing, accountability, and community involvement, the book seeks to inspire readers to embrace restorative practices in their own lives and communities, ultimately contributing to a more just and compassionate society.

Structure of the Book

This book, "The Philosophy of Restorative Justice," is designed to provide a comprehensive and in-depth exploration of restorative justice, from its philosophical foundations to its practical applications and transformative potential. To guide readers through this complex and multifaceted subject, the book is organized into ten chapters, each focusing on a specific aspect of restorative justice. This structure ensures a thorough understanding of the concepts, principles, and real-world implementations of restorative justice.

Chapter 1: Historical Foundations of Restorative Justice

The first chapter delves into the historical roots of restorative justice, tracing its origins from ancient practices to its modern resurgence. It covers:

1. Ancient Practices: An exploration of restorative justice in ancient cultures, including examples from indigenous societies that emphasize community-based conflict resolution.

2. Medieval and Early Modern Periods: How justice systems evolved during these periods, incorporating elements of restorative practices.

3. Modern Resurgence: The revival of restorative justice in the 20th and 21st centuries, driven by a growing recognition of its benefits over purely punitive systems.

Chapter 2: Theoretical Frameworks

Chapter two examines the philosophical and theoretical foundations of restorative justice. It includes:

1. Philosophical Underpinnings: An analysis of key philosophical theories that support restorative justice, such as relational ethics, communitarianism, virtue ethics, and restorative ontology.

2. Ethical Considerations: A discussion on morality, ethics, and the philosophy of punishment as they relate to restorative justice.

3. Restorative vs. Retributive Justice: A comparative study of restorative and retributive justice models, highlighting their differences and complementarities.

Chapter 3: Core Principles and Values

The third chapter focuses on the core principles and values that underpin restorative justice. It covers:

. Accountability: The role of taking responsibility in restorative justice and its importance in the healing process.

2. Reparation: The concept of making amends and repairing harm caused by wrongdoing.

3. Community Involvement: The significance of involving the community in the justice process.

4. Empathy and Healing: How fostering empathy and emotional healing contributes to the effectiveness of restorative justice.

Chapter 4: Restorative Practices and Models

Chapter four provides a detailed examination of various restorative justice practices and models, including:

1. Victim-Offender Mediation: The process and benefits of direct mediation between victims and offenders.

2. Family Group Conferencing: The involvement of family and community members in resolving conflicts.

3. Circle Processes: The role of restorative circles in facilitating open dialogue and mutual understanding.

4. Community Restorative Boards: Community-driven initiatives that focus on resolving conflicts and repairing harm.

Chapter 5: Case Studies and Real-World Applications

The fifth chapter highlights practical applications of restorative justice through case studies and real-world examples. It includes:

1. Criminal Justice System: How restorative justice is implemented within criminal justice systems and its impact on reducing recidivism.

2. Schools and Educational Settings: The application of restorative justice in schools and its effects on student behavior and academic outcomes.

3. Workplace and Organizations: Restorative approaches to resolving workplace conflicts and improving organizational culture.

4. Community Programs: Examples of successful community-based restorative justice programs and their outcomes.

Chapter 6: Benefits and Challenges

Chapter six discusses the benefits and challenges associated with restorative justice. It covers:

1. Positive Outcomes: Evidence of the benefits of restorative justice for victims, offenders, and communities.

2. Common Challenges: Obstacles to implementing restorative justice and strategies to overcome them.

3. Criticisms and Controversies: Addressing criticisms and debating contentious issues surrounding restorative justice.

Chapter 7: Restorative Justice and the Legal System

The seventh chapter explores the integration of restorative justice within traditional legal systems. It includes:

1. Integration with Traditional Justice: How restorative justice can complement and enhance traditional legal frameworks.

2. Legislative Frameworks: Laws and policies that support restorative justice.

3. Case Law and Precedents: Notable legal cases and their implications for the development and implementation of restorative justice.

Chapter 8: Restorative Justice in International Contexts

Chapter eight provides a global perspective on restorative justice practices. It covers:

1. Global Perspectives: An overview of restorative justice practices around the world.

2. Transitional Justice: The role of restorative justice in post-conflict and transitional societies.

3. Human Rights and Restorative Justice: The relationship between restorative justice and human rights principles.

Chapter 9: Restorative Justice and Social Justice

The ninth chapter examines the intersection of restorative justice with social justice issues. It includes:

1. Intersectionality: Addressing issues of race, gender, and class in restorative justice practices.

2. Social Equity: Promoting fairness and equality through restorative justice.

3. Community Empowerment: How restorative justice fosters stronger, more resilient communities.

Chapter 10: The Future of Restorative Justice

The final chapter speculates on the future directions and innovations in restorative justice. It covers:

1. Innovations and Trends: Emerging trends and new approaches in restorative justice.

2. Sustainability and Scalability: Ensuring the long-term success and broader adoption of restorative practices.

3. Vision for the Future: A visionary look at the potential of restorative justice to transform societies and create a more just world.

Conclusion

In conclusion, this book provides a comprehensive exploration of restorative justice, offering insights into its philosophical foundations, practical applications, and transformative potential. By delving into the historical roots, core principles, real-world applications, and future possibilities of restorative justice, the book aims to inspire readers to embrace and advocate for restorative practices in their own lives and communities. Through understanding and applying restorative justice, we can work towards a more just, compassionate, and harmonious society.

DR. MAXWELL SHIMBA

HISTORICAL FOUNDATIONS OF RESTORATIVE JUSTICE

What is Philosophy?

Philosophy is the study of fundamental questions concerning existence, knowledge, values, reason, mind, and language. It involves critical examination and systematic approaches to understanding the world and our place within it. Philosophy seeks to uncover truths through reasoned argument, introspection, and dialogue, rather than relying solely on empirical evidence. It addresses a wide array of subjects, from metaphysics and epistemology to ethics and political philosophy, providing a framework for examining complex issues and developing coherent viewpoints.

Philosophy is divided into several branches:

1. Metaphysics: The study of the nature of reality, existence, and the universe.

2. Epistemology: The investigation of the nature and scope of knowledge and belief.

3. Ethics: The exploration of moral values, principles, and rules that govern human conduct.

4. Aesthetics: The study of beauty, art, and taste.

5. Logic: The analysis of valid reasoning and argument structure.

6. Political Philosophy: The examination of government, justice, rights, and the role of individuals within a society.

Philosophy serves as the foundation for critical thinking and rational analysis, influencing various fields including science, law, and theology. It helps in understanding and addressing fundamental human concerns, shaping how we view the world and our interactions within it.

Philosophy and Restorative Justice

The relationship between philosophy and restorative justice is profound and multifaceted. Restorative justice, as a practice and ideology, is deeply rooted in several philosophical principles and traditions that emphasize the importance of relationships, community, and ethical responsibility. Understanding the philosophical underpinnings of restorative justice provides clarity and depth to its principles and practices.

1. Relational Ethics

Interconnectedness: Relational ethics is a philosophical approach that emphasizes the interconnectedness of individuals within a community. It asserts that our moral obligations are grounded in the relationships we have with others.

- Restorative Justice Application: In restorative justice, this interconnectedness is acknowledged through practices that involve victims, offenders, and the community. The goal is to repair the harm caused by an offense and to restore the relationships disrupted by it.

2. Communitarianism

- Community Values: Communitarianism is a philosophical perspective that stresses the importance of community values and the collective well-being of society.

- Restorative Justice Application: Restorative justice aligns with communitarianism by prioritizing the restoration of community harmony. It involves the community in the justice process, recognizing that crime affects not only the individuals directly involved but also the broader community.

3. Virtue Ethics

- Moral Character: Virtue ethics, rooted in Aristotelian philosophy, focuses on the development of moral character and virtues such as empathy, compassion, and responsibility.

- Restorative Justice Application: Restorative justice practices encourage the cultivation of these virtues in both victims and offenders. Through dialogue and accountability, individuals are guided towards moral growth and ethical behavior.

4. Restorative Ontology

- Need for Restoration: Restorative ontology is a philosophical approach that underscores the fundamental need for restoration and healing in the aftermath of harm.

- Restorative Justice Application: This perspective posits that true justice can only be achieved when relationships are mended and communities are strengthened. Restorative justice practices focus on addressing the harm caused and finding ways to make amends, promoting healing for all parties involved.

5. Ethical Responsibility

- Moral Duty: The philosophy of ethical responsibility highlights the moral duty individuals have to address the harm they cause and to contribute positively to their communities.

- Restorative Justice Application: Restorative justice emphasizes accountability and the active participation of offenders in making amends. It fosters a sense of moral duty and encourages individuals to take responsibility for their actions.

Historical Foundations of Restorative Justice

The historical foundations of restorative justice can be traced back to ancient practices and traditional justice systems around the world. These practices were often community-based, focusing on repairing harm and restoring harmony within societies. Understanding the historical context of restorative justice provides insight into its enduring principles and the reasons for its resurgence in modern times.

1. Ancient Practices

- Indigenous Traditions: Many indigenous cultures have long utilized restorative approaches to justice. For example, Native American tribes practiced community-based dispute-resolution processes that emphasized healing, community involvement, and the reintegration of offenders into society.

- African Justice Systems: Traditional justice systems in Africa, such as the Gacaca courts in Rwanda, focused on reconciliation and community healing. These systems prioritized repairing relationships and restoring social harmony.

- Maori Practices in New Zealand: The Maori people of New Zealand have a rich history of restorative justice practices, which have significantly influenced the country's modern justice system. The Family Group Conference, a cornerstone of New Zealand's restorative justice approach, originated from Maori traditions.

2. Medieval and Early Modern Periods

- Community Justice in Europe: During the medieval period, many European communities practiced forms of restorative justice. Local courts often prioritized reconciliation and restitution over punitive measures.

- Early Modern Developments: The early modern period saw the evolution of justice systems, with some elements of restorative practices being integrated into legal frameworks. However, the rise of centralized states and formal legal systems gradually shifted the focus towards retributive justice.

3. Modern Resurgence

- 20th Century Revival: The 20th century witnessed a resurgence of interest in restorative justice, driven by growing dissatisfaction with traditional punitive systems. Scholars, activists, and practitioners began to advocate for approaches that emphasized healing and community involvement.

- Influential Figures: Key figures in the restorative justice movement, such as Howard Zehr, played a crucial role in articulating and promoting restorative principles. Zehr's work, including his seminal book "Changing Lenses," helped to define and popularize restorative justice.

- Global Adoption: In recent decades, restorative justice has gained recognition and adoption in various sectors, including criminal justice, education, workplaces, and communities. Countries around the world have implemented restorative practices, reflecting a growing acknowledgment of their effectiveness and transformative potential.

Conclusion

Philosophy provides the foundation for understanding the principles and practices of restorative justice. Through the lens of relational ethics, communitarianism, virtue ethics, restorative ontology, and ethical responsibility, restorative justice emerges as a deeply rooted and philosophically sound approach to addressing harm and conflict. By tracing its historical foundations from ancient practices to its modern resurgence, we gain a comprehensive understanding of the enduring values and transformative potential of restorative justice. This chapter sets the stage for a deeper exploration of restorative justice in the chapters that follow, as we delve into its core principles, practical applications, and future directions.

Ancient Practices: Restorative Justice in Ancient Cultures and Societies

Restorative justice, while often considered a modern innovation, has deep roots in ancient cultures and societies. These early practices emphasized community harmony, reconciliation, and the restoration of relationships. This chapter explores the rich tapestry of restorative justice traditions across different civilizations, demonstrating how these ancient practices have influenced contemporary approaches to justice.

Indigenous Traditions

Native American Tribes

Among Native American tribes, justice was traditionally community-based and focused on healing rather than punishment. Tribal societies viewed crime as a disruption of the social fabric, necessitating efforts to restore balance and harmony. Some key aspects of Native American restorative justice practices included:

- Peacemaking Circles: Also known as talking circles, these gatherings allowed community members to speak openly and honestly about the harm caused by an offense. The goal was to foster understanding, accountability, and collective healing. Everyone, including the victim, offender, and community members, had an opportunity to share their perspectives.

- Mediation by Elders: Elders often played a crucial role as mediators, using their wisdom and authority to guide the process of reconciliation. Their involvement lent legitimacy to the proceedings and helped ensure that the outcomes were respected and upheld by the community.

- Focus on Relationships: Native American justice emphasized the restoration of relationships over retribution. Offenders were encouraged to understand the impact of their actions, make amends, and reintegrate into the community.

African Justice Systems

In many African societies, traditional justice systems were inherently restorative, focusing on reconciliation and the reintegration of offenders. The principles of restorative justice were embedded in various cultural practices and communal structures.

- Gacaca Courts in Rwanda: The Gacaca courts are a notable example of restorative justice in Africa. These community-based courts were revitalized after the 1994 Rwandan genocide to address the overwhelming number of genocide-related cases. The process involved public hearings where perpetrators confessed their crimes, apologized, and sought forgiveness from their victims and the community.

The emphasis was on truth-telling, accountability, and rebuilding social harmony.

- Ubuntu Philosophy: The concept of Ubuntu, prevalent in many African cultures, underscores the interconnectedness of all people. It holds that an individual's humanity is intertwined with the humanity of others. In the context of justice, this philosophy translates into practices that seek to restore communal bonds and promote collective well-being. Justice is achieved not through punishment but through restoring harmony and ensuring that offenders understand their responsibilities to the community.

Maori Practices in New Zealand

The Maori people of New Zealand have a long history of restorative justice practices that have significantly influenced the country's modern justice system. Maori traditions emphasize collective responsibility, reconciliation, and the restoration of balance.

- Family Group Conferences (FGCs): FGCs are rooted in Maori customs and have become a cornerstone of New Zealand's restorative justice approach. These conferences bring together the victim, offender, their families, and community members to discuss the harm caused and agree on a plan for making amends. The process emphasizes consensus-building and collective decision-making.

- Tikanga Maori: Tikanga Maori, or Maori customary law, provides a framework for resolving conflicts that prioritizes the restoration of relationships and the well-being of the community. It incorporates practices such as hui (meetings) and korero (discussions) to address harm and find solutions that benefit all parties involved.

Ancient Justice Systems

Early Middle Eastern Practices

Ancient Middle Eastern societies also practiced forms of restorative justice. The Code of Hammurabi, one of the earliest known legal codes from ancient Babylon, included provisions for restitution and compensation. While it is often cited for its retributive aspects ("an eye for an eye"), it also emphasizes the importance of restoring balance through compensation to victims.

- Restitution: Offenders were required to compensate their victims for the harm caused. This compensation could take the form of goods, services, or money, depending on the nature of the offense. The focus was on making the victim whole again and restoring social harmony.

Ancient Greece

In ancient Greece, justice was often a communal affair, with citizens playing an active role in resolving disputes. Restorative elements were evident in their approach to justice, particularly in the emphasis on reconciliation and compensation.

- Athenian Democracy: In Athens, the legal system allowed for public participation in the administration of justice. Citizens could bring cases to public courts, and juries composed of ordinary citizens would decide the outcomes. This participatory approach fostered a sense of collective responsibility and accountability.

- Amphictyonic League: The Amphictyonic League, a religious association of Greek tribes, administered justice through councils that sought to resolve conflicts and restore peace. This league's practices emphasized mediation and reconciliation, reflecting restorative justice principles.

Ancient Rome

Roman law also incorporated restorative elements, particularly in its approach to property crimes and personal injury. The Twelve Tables, the earliest attempt to codify Roman law, included provisions for restitution and compensation.

- Lex Aquilia: The Lex Aquilia was a Roman law that provided compensation for wrongful damage to property. It established the principle that offenders should compensate victims for their losses, reflecting a restorative approach to justice.

- Paterfamilias: In cases of familial disputes, the head of the family, or paterfamilias, often acted as a mediator, seeking to resolve conflicts within the household and restore harmony.

Ancient Asian Practices

Confucianism in China

Confucianism, a dominant philosophical and ethical system in ancient China, emphasized the importance of social harmony, familial duty, and moral rectitude. These principles were reflected in the justice practices of the time.

- Mediation and Reconciliation: Confucian justice prioritized mediation and reconciliation over punishment. Local magistrates often acted as mediators, seeking to resolve disputes through dialogue and mutual agreement. The goal was to restore harmony and maintain social order.

- Filial Piety: The Confucian value of filial piety, or respect for one's parents and ancestors, extended to a broader respect for social relationships. Justice practices aimed to reinforce these relationships and ensure that offenders fulfilled their moral obligations to their families and communities.

Hindu and Buddhist Traditions in India

In ancient India, Hindu and Buddhist traditions influenced justice practices that emphasized karma, dharma, and the resolution of conflict through ethical conduct and reconciliation.

- Panchayat System: The Panchayat system, a traditional village council, played a crucial role in administering justice in rural India. These councils aimed to resolve disputes through consensus and mediation, focusing on restoring harmony within the community.

- Buddhist Teachings: Buddhist teachings on compassion, non-violence, and the interconnectedness of all beings informed justice practices that prioritized reconciliation and the restoration of balance. Monastic communities often served as mediators in disputes, seeking to guide parties toward peaceful resolution.

Conclusion

The ancient practices of restorative justice in diverse cultures and societies demonstrate the universality and timelessness of restorative principles. These early traditions emphasized community involvement, reconciliation, and the restoration of relationships, laying the groundwork for contemporary restorative justice practices. By understanding the historical foundations of restorative justice, we gain insight into its enduring values and transformative potential, setting the stage for further exploration of its core principles and modern applications in the chapters that follow.

Medieval and Early Modern Periods: Evolution of Justice Systems and Restorative Practices

The medieval and early modern periods were marked by significant developments in justice systems and the evolution of restorative practices. These eras witnessed a gradual shift from community-based justice systems to more centralized and formal legal frameworks. However, elements of restorative justice persisted, often intertwined with retributive justice approaches. This chapter explores how justice systems evolved during these periods and highlights the restorative practices that continued to play a crucial role in maintaining social harmony.

Medieval Period

Community-Based Justice

During the medieval period, justice was predominantly administered at the local level, with communities playing a central role in resolving disputes and maintaining order. Key aspects of community-based justice include:

- Manorial Courts: In medieval Europe, manorial courts were a primary means of administering justice. These courts were presided over by local lords and addressed various disputes within the manor, such as land conflicts, breaches of contract, and minor criminal offenses. The focus was often on restoring relationships and ensuring the smooth functioning of the community.

- Tithing and Frankpledge Systems: These systems required groups of households to take collective responsibility for each other's behavior. If a member of the group committed a crime, the entire group was responsible for ensuring the offender faced justice and made amends. This communal approach emphasized accountability and restitution.

- Church Courts: The Church played a significant role in the justice system, particularly in matters of moral and religious conduct. Church courts, or ecclesiastical courts, handled issues such as marriage disputes, wills, and breaches of faith. These courts often emphasized penance, reconciliation, and the restoration of spiritual harmony.

Restorative Practices

Despite the prevalence of retributive justice, restorative practices were still integral to medieval justice systems. Some notable restorative elements included:

- Wergild: In Germanic law, the concept of wergild (man price) required offenders to compensate victims or their families for harm caused. This practice aimed to prevent blood feuds and restore social harmony by providing a structured means of reparation.

- Trial by Ordeal and Compurgation: While these practices may not seem restorative by modern standards, they often involved community participation and sought to resolve disputes through methods perceived as fair and just by contemporary society. Compurgation, for example, involved oaths from community members attesting to a person's character and truthfulness.

- Public Apology and Reconciliation: Public apologies and acts of penance were common in resolving disputes and offenses. These acts aimed to acknowledge wrongdoing, seek forgiveness, and restore relationships within the community.

Early Modern Period

The early modern period saw the gradual centralization and formalization of justice systems. National governments began to exert greater control over legal processes, leading to the development of more standardized and bureaucratic justice systems. However, restorative practices continued to exist alongside these changes.

Centralization of Justice

- Rise of Nation-States: The emergence of nation-states brought about centralized legal systems. Monarchs and central governments established courts and legal codes to standardize justice across their realms. This centralization aimed to reduce local variations in justice and ensure more consistent application of laws.

- Professionalization of the Judiciary: The early modern period witnessed the professionalization of the judiciary, with the establishment of trained judges and lawyers. This development contributed to a more formal and structured approach to justice, often emphasizing retributive measures.

- Codification of Laws: Legal codes, such as the Napoleonic Code in France, were developed to provide clear and comprehensive legal frameworks. These codes sought to standardize justice and reduce arbitrary rulings.

Persistence of Restorative Practices

Despite the trend towards centralization and formalization, restorative practices persisted in various forms during the early modern period. Key examples include:

- Community Mediation and Arbitration: Local communities continued to play a role in resolving disputes through mediation and arbitration. Community leaders and respected individuals often acted as mediators, seeking to find mutually acceptable solutions and restore harmony.

- Restitution and Compensation: The principle of restitution remained important in early modern justice systems. Offenders were frequently required to compensate victims for their losses, reflecting a restorative approach to justice.

- Reconciliation Rituals: Rituals of reconciliation, such as public apologies, acts of contrition, and ceremonies of forgiveness, continued to be used to address harm and restore relationships. These rituals were often deeply embedded in local customs and traditions.

Influence of Enlightenment Thought

The Enlightenment, a period of intellectual and philosophical growth in the 17th and 18th centuries, brought new perspectives on justice and human rights. Enlightenment thinkers such as John Locke, Jean-Jacques Rousseau, and Cesare Beccaria influenced the evolution of justice systems with their ideas on individual rights, social contracts, and rational-legal principles.

- Human Rights and Justice: Enlightenment thought emphasized the importance of individual rights and the need for justice systems to protect these rights. This perspective contributed to the development of legal frameworks that sought to balance retributive and restorative elements.

- Rational and Proportional Punishment: Cesare Beccaria's work, "On Crimes and Punishments," argued for rational and proportional punishment, emphasizing that penalties should be designed to prevent future crimes and promote societal well-being. Beccaria's ideas helped shift justice systems towards more humane and rational approaches, incorporating restorative principles of fairness and proportionality.

Case Studies and Examples

England: The Assize Courts and Local Justice

In England, the Assize Courts were established to administer justice across the country. These traveling courts brought royal justice to local communities, addressing serious criminal cases. Despite the formalization of justice, local customs and restorative practices continued to influence legal proceedings.

- The Role of Juries: Juries, composed of local community members, played a significant role in the Assize Courts. Their participation ensured that local knowledge and community values were considered in the administration of justice.

- Settlement of Disputes: Local communities often settle minor disputes through informal means, such as arbitration and mediation by community elders, reflecting restorative practices.

Colonial America: Hybrid Justice Systems

In colonial America, justice systems combined elements of English common law with local customs and practices. This hybrid approach allowed for the incorporation of restorative elements in the administration of justice.

- Town Meetings and Community Mediation: Town meetings and community assemblies were common in colonial America, providing forums for resolving disputes and addressing community issues. These gatherings emphasized collective decision-making and the restoration of social harmony.

- Restitution and Compensation: Colonial justice systems frequently required offenders to make restitution to their victims, reflecting the influence of restorative principles.

Conclusion

The medieval and early modern periods were marked by significant changes in justice systems, with a gradual shift towards centralization and formalization. However, restorative practices continued to play a crucial role in maintaining social harmony and addressing harm. Community-based justice, restitution, public apologies, and reconciliation rituals persisted alongside more formal legal frameworks, reflecting the enduring value of restorative principles. Understanding these historical developments provides a foundation for appreciating the evolution of restorative justice and its relevance in contemporary society. In the chapters that follow, we will explore the philosophical foundations, core principles, practical applications, and transformative potential of restorative justice, building on the rich historical context outlined in this chapter.

Modern Resurgence: The Revival of Restorative Justice in the 20th and 21st Centuries

The modern resurgence of restorative justice represents a significant shift in how societies address crime and conflict. After centuries dominated by retributive justice models, the 20th and 21st centuries have seen a renewed interest in restorative practices that emphasize healing, accountability, and community involvement. This chapter explores the key factors contributing to this revival, the influential figures and movements, and the widespread adoption of restorative justice across various sectors.

Factors Contributing to the Modern Resurgence

Several factors have contributed to the revival of restorative justice in the modern era:

1. Dissatisfaction with Retributive Justice

- High Recidivism Rates: Traditional punitive systems often fail to rehabilitate offenders, leading to high rates of recidivism. This has prompted a search for more effective approaches to reducing crime and promoting rehabilitation.

- Victim Dissatisfaction: Victims of crime frequently feel neglected and unsatisfied with retributive justice systems, which focus primarily on punishing offenders rather than addressing victims' needs for healing and restitution.

- Community Impact: Communities impacted by crime often feel left out of the justice process, leading to a sense of disempowerment and disengagement. Restorative justice offers a more inclusive approach that involves the community in finding solutions.

2. Emerging Theoretical and Empirical Support

- Criminological Research: Studies in criminology have highlighted the limitations of punitive approaches and the potential benefits of restorative practices in reducing reoffending and promoting social harmony.

- Psychological Insights: Psychological research has underscored the importance of addressing the emotional and relational aspects of crime, supporting the restorative emphasis on empathy, accountability, and reconciliation.

- Human Rights Advocacy: Human rights movements have advocated for justice systems that respect the dignity and rights of all individuals, including offenders, victims, and community members.

3. Influential Social Movements

- Civil Rights Movements: Civil rights movements in the mid-20th century challenged systemic injustices and advocated for more equitable and humane approaches to justice.

- Peace and Reconciliation Efforts: Post-conflict reconciliation efforts, such as those in South Africa after apartheid, demonstrated the power of restorative approaches in healing deep societal wounds and rebuilding trust.

Key Figures and Movements

Several influential figures and movements have played pivotal roles in the modern resurgence of restorative justice:

1. Howard Zehr

- Pioneering Work: Often referred to as the "grandfather of restorative justice," Howard Zehr's work has been instrumental in defining and promoting restorative justice principles. His seminal book, "Changing Lenses: A New Focus for Crime and Justice," published in 1990, articulated a vision for a justice system that prioritizes healing over punishment.

- Restorative Justice Philosophy: Zehr's philosophy emphasizes the importance of repairing harm, involving all stakeholders in the justice process, and transforming relationships affected by crime. His work has inspired practitioners, policymakers, and scholars worldwide.

2. Victim-Offender Reconciliation Programs (VORP)

- Early Initiatives: One of the earliest modern restorative justice programs, VORP, began in Kitchener, Ontario, Canada, in the 1970s. The program facilitated direct meetings between victims and offenders, allowing them to discuss the harm caused and agree on ways to make amends.

- Global Influence: The success of VORP led to the establishment of similar programs in North America, Europe, and beyond, demonstrating the effectiveness of restorative practices in addressing harm and fostering reconciliation.

3. Truth and Reconciliation Commissions (TRCs)

- South Africa's TRC: One of the most notable examples of restorative justice in practice is South Africa's Truth and Reconciliation Commission, established in 1995 to address the atrocities committed during apartheid. The TRC focused on truth-telling, accountability, and reconciliation, providing a platform for victims and perpetrators to share their stories and seek forgiveness.

- Global Impact: The TRC model has influenced numerous other countries dealing with post-conflict reconciliation, including Rwanda, Canada, and Sierra Leone, highlighting the transformative potential of restorative justice in healing divided societies.

Adoption and Implementation Across Sectors

The revival of restorative justice has led to its adoption and implementation across various sectors, including criminal justice, education, workplaces, and communities:

1. Criminal Justice System

- Diversion Programs: Restorative justice is increasingly used as a diversionary measure for juvenile and adult offenders, providing an alternative to traditional prosecution and incarceration. These programs focus on accountability, restitution, and rehabilitation.

- Restorative Practices in Prisons: Some prisons have incorporated restorative practices to address conflicts, promote rehabilitation, and prepare inmates for reintegration into society. Programs such as victim-offender dialogues and restorative circles have shown positive outcomes in reducing recidivism and improving inmate behavior.

2. Educational Settings

- Restorative School Discipline: Schools have adopted restorative practices to address disciplinary issues, improve school climate, and reduce suspensions and expulsions. Restorative circles, peer mediation, and restorative conferences are used to resolve conflicts and build positive relationships among students and staff.

- Preventive Measures: Restorative practices in schools also serve as preventive measures, fostering a culture of respect, empathy, and accountability that helps prevent bullying and other harmful behaviors.

3. Workplaces

- Conflict Resolution: Restorative justice principles are applied in workplace settings to resolve conflicts, improve communication, and build a positive organizational culture. Mediation and facilitated dialogues help address grievances and restore harmony.

- Promoting Inclusivity: Restorative practices in the workplace promote inclusivity and collaboration, encouraging employees to take responsibility for their actions and contribute to a supportive work environment.

4. Community Programs

- Community Restorative Justice: Community-based restorative justice programs address various issues, from neighborhood disputes to serious criminal offenses. These programs involve community members in the justice process, fostering a sense of collective responsibility and empowerment.

- Restorative Cities: Some cities have embraced restorative justice principles at a municipal level, integrating restorative practices into local governance, policing, and community services. These initiatives aim to create more cohesive and resilient communities.

The Impact and Future of Restorative Justice

The modern resurgence of restorative justice has had a profound impact on justice systems and communities worldwide. Its emphasis on healing, accountability, and community involvement offers a transformative alternative to punitive approaches. The following sections explore the impact of restorative justice and its potential future directions:

1. Impact on Victims

- Empowerment: Restorative justice empowers victims by giving them a voice in the justice process and addressing their needs for healing and closure. Victims report higher levels of satisfaction and a greater sense of justice compared to traditional retributive systems.

- Healing and Recovery: The opportunity to communicate with offenders, express their feelings, and receive restitution helps victims heal and move forward.

2. Impact on Offenders

- Accountability and Rehabilitation: Restorative justice encourages offenders to take responsibility for their actions, understand the impact of their behavior, and actively participate in making amends. This process promotes personal growth and reduces the likelihood of reoffending.

- Reintegration: By involving the community in the justice process, restorative justice facilitates the reintegration of offenders, helping them rebuild positive relationships and become productive members of society.

3. Impact on Communities

- Strengthening Social Bonds: Restorative justice fosters stronger social bonds and a sense of collective responsibility. Communities become more resilient and better equipped to address conflicts and prevent crime.

- Building Trust: The inclusive and participatory nature of restorative justice helps build trust between community members, law enforcement, and the justice system.

4. Future Directions

- Expansion and Integration: The future of restorative justice lies in its continued expansion and integration into various sectors. Policymakers, practitioners, and advocates are working to embed restorative practices within legal frameworks, educational policies, and community programs.

- Research and Innovation: Ongoing research and innovation are crucial to understanding the full potential of restorative justice. Studies on the long-term outcomes of restorative practices, the development of new models, and the exploration of restorative justice in diverse cultural contexts will contribute to its evolution and effectiveness.

- Global Movement: The global movement for restorative justice is gaining momentum, with international networks and organizations promoting restorative principles and practices. Collaborative efforts and knowledge-sharing will continue to drive the growth and impact of restorative justice worldwide.

Conclusion

The modern resurgence of restorative justice in the 20th and 21st centuries represents a significant shift towards more humane, effective, and inclusive approaches to addressing crime and conflict. Influenced by dissatisfaction with retributive justice, emerging theoretical and empirical support, and influential social movements, restorative justice has gained widespread adoption across various sectors. The contributions of key figures, such as Howard Zehr, and the success of initiatives like victim-offender reconciliation programs and truth and reconciliation commissions have demonstrated the transformative potential of restorative justice. As we move forward, the continued expansion, integration, and innovation of restorative practices will shape the future of justice systems and contribute to building more just and compassionate societies. In the chapters that follow, we will delve deeper into the philosophical foundations, core principles, practical applications, and transformative impact of restorative justice, building on the rich historical context outlined in this chapter.

CHAPTER 02

THEORETICAL FRAMEWORKS

Philosophical Underpinnings: Key Philosophical Theories that Support Restorative Justice

Restorative justice is grounded in a rich tapestry of philosophical theories that emphasize the importance of relationships, community, and ethical responsibility. These theories provide the intellectual and moral foundations for restorative practices, guiding principles, and the pursuit of justice that heals rather than harms. This chapter explores the key philosophical theories that underpin restorative justice, offering insights into how these ideas shape and inform restorative practices.

Relational Ethics

Relational ethics is a philosophical approach that emphasizes the interconnectedness of individuals within a community. It asserts that our moral obligations are grounded in the relationships we have with others and that ethical behavior involves maintaining and restoring these relationships.

1. Interconnectedness of Individuals

- Relational Nature of Humanity: Relational ethics posits that human beings are inherently relational creatures. Our identities, actions, and well-being are deeply interconnected with those of others.

- Moral Obligations: Our moral responsibilities arise from the relationships we share with others. This perspective shifts the focus from individual actions to the broader context of social interactions and communal bonds.

2. Restorative Justice Application

- Healing Relationships: Restorative justice seeks to repair the harm caused by crime by focusing on the restoration of relationships between victims, offenders, and the community. It recognizes that crime disrupts social bonds and that justice involves healing these rifts.

- Community Involvement: By involving the community in the justice process, restorative justice acknowledges the interconnectedness of individuals and the collective responsibility for maintaining social harmony.

Communitarianism

Communitarianism is a philosophical perspective that stresses the importance of community values and the collective well-being of society. It emphasizes that individuals are shaped by their communities and that a just society prioritizes the common good.

1. Community Values and the Common Good

- Social Fabric: Communitarianism views society as a complex web of relationships, where the well-being of individuals is intertwined with the health of the community.

- Collective Responsibility: It advocates for a sense of collective responsibility, where community members work together to uphold shared values and address issues that affect the common good.

2. Restorative Justice Application

- Restoring Community Harmony: Restorative justice aligns with communitarianism by prioritizing the restoration of community harmony. It involves the community in the justice process, recognizing that crime affects not only the individuals directly involved but also the broader social fabric.

- Collective Decision-Making: Restorative practices often involve collective decision-making, where community members, victims, and offenders collaborate to find solutions that promote the common good and restore social equilibrium.

Virtue Ethics

Virtue ethics, rooted in Aristotelian philosophy, focuses on the development of moral character and virtues such as empathy, compassion, and responsibility. It emphasizes the cultivation of good character traits that enable individuals to live ethical and fulfilling lives.

1. Moral Character and Virtues

- The Good Life: Virtue ethics posits that the good life is achieved through the cultivation of virtues, which are habitual dispositions to act in morally excellent ways.

- Role of Community: The development of virtues is supported by the community, which provides the context for moral growth and the reinforcement of ethical behavior.

2. Restorative Justice Application

- Fostering Empathy and Compassion: Restorative justice practices encourage the cultivation of empathy, compassion, and responsibility in both victims and offenders. Through dialogue and accountability, individuals are guided towards moral growth and ethical behavior.

- Character Development: By focusing on the rehabilitation of offenders and the healing of victims, restorative justice promotes the development of virtues that contribute to personal and social well-being.

Restorative Ontology

Restorative ontology is a philosophical approach that underscores the fundamental need for restoration and healing in the aftermath of harm. It posits that true justice can only be achieved when relationships are mended and communities are strengthened.

1. The Need for Restoration

- Ontological Harm: Restorative ontology recognizes that harm affects the very being of individuals and communities. It disrupts relationships, trust, and social cohesion.

- Restorative Imperative: The imperative to restore is rooted in the recognition that justice involves more than punishment; it requires the active repair of the damage caused by wrongdoing.

2. Restorative Justice Application

- Repairing Harm: Restorative justice is fundamentally about repairing harm. It seeks to address the needs of victims, hold offenders accountable in constructive ways, and restore relationships affected by crime.

- Strengthening Communities: By focusing on restoration, restorative justice strengthens communities, building resilience and fostering a culture of care and mutual support.

Ethical Responsibility

The philosophy of ethical responsibility highlights the moral duty individuals have to address the harm they cause and to contribute positively to their communities. It emphasizes accountability, restitution, and the ethical imperative to make amends.

1. Moral Duty and Accountability

- Ethical Accountability: Ethical responsibility involves acknowledging the impact of one's actions on others and taking steps to make things right. It is rooted in the moral duty to act justly and responsibly.

- Restitution and Reparation: Addressing harm through restitution and reparation is a key aspect of ethical responsibility. It involves making amends and taking concrete actions to repair the damage caused.

2. Restorative Justice Application

- Promoting Accountability: Restorative justice emphasizes accountability by encouraging offenders to take responsibility for their actions and actively participate in making amends. This process fosters a sense of ethical responsibility and moral duty.

- Fulfilling Moral Obligations: By addressing the needs of victims and the community, restorative justice helps individuals fulfill their moral obligations and contribute positively to the well-being of society.

Dialogical Ethics

Dialogical ethics, influenced by philosophers such as Martin Buber and Jürgen Habermas, emphasizes the importance of dialogue and communication in ethical decision-making. It posits that ethical understanding and mutual respect arise from open and honest dialogue.

1. Ethics of Dialogue

- I-Thou Relationship: Martin Buber's concept of the I-Thou relationship emphasizes the importance of seeing others as whole persons and engaging with them in genuine, respectful dialogue.

- Communicative Action: Jürgen Habermas's theory of communicative action highlights the role of rational dialogue in achieving mutual understanding and consensus. Ethical norms are established through open, inclusive, and reasoned communication.

2. Restorative Justice Application

- Facilitating Dialogue: Restorative justice practices, such as restorative circles and victim-offender mediation, facilitate dialogue between victims, offenders, and community members. This dialogue fosters mutual understanding, respect, and collaborative problem-solving.

-       Building   Consensus: By   prioritizing communication and dialogue, restorative justice helps build consensus and shared ethical understanding among all stakeholders involved in the justice process.

Conclusion

The philosophical underpinnings of restorative justice provide a robust framework for understanding its principles and practices. Relational ethics, communitarianism, virtue ethics, restorative ontology, ethical responsibility, and dialogical ethics collectively emphasize the importance of relationships, community, and ethical behavior in achieving justice. These philosophical theories guide restorative justice in its pursuit of healing, accountability, and the restoration of social harmony. In the chapters that follow, we will delve deeper into the core principles, practical applications, and transformative potential of restorative justice, building on the philosophical foundations outlined in this chapter.

Ethical Considerations: Morality, Ethics, and the Philosophy of Punishment

The ethical considerations surrounding restorative justice are deeply rooted in questions of morality, the nature of ethical behavior, and the philosophy of punishment. This chapter explores these themes, examining how they inform and shape restorative justice practices. By understanding the ethical foundations of restorative justice, we gain insight into its moral imperatives and the ways it seeks to address harm, promote accountability, and restore community harmony.

Morality and Ethics

Morality and ethics are foundational concepts that guide human behavior and decision-making. While often used interchangeably, they have distinct meanings and implications in the context of restorative justice.

1. Morality

   - Definition: Morality refers to the principles and values that individuals and societies hold regarding what is right and wrong, good and bad. These principles guide behavior and form the basis for moral judgments.

   - Sources of Morality: Morality can be derived from various sources, including religious beliefs, cultural norms, personal values, and philosophical reasoning. It shapes our understanding of justice, responsibility, and ethical conduct.

2. Ethics

   - Definition: Ethics is the systematic study of moral principles, examining how they apply to specific situations and guiding decision-making processes. It involves critical reflection on what constitutes right action and the justification for moral choices.

- Branches of Ethics: Ethics is divided into several branches, including normative ethics (which explores moral standards and principles), applied ethics (which addresses specific ethical issues), and meta-ethics (which examines the nature and meaning of ethical terms and concepts).

The Philosophy of Punishment

The philosophy of punishment addresses the reasons and justifications for imposing penalties on individuals who commit wrongdoing. It explores various theories of punishment and their ethical implications.

1. Retributive Justice

- Definition: Retributive justice is based on the principle of "just deserts," which holds that individuals should be punished in proportion to the severity of their offenses. It emphasizes retribution and moral accountability.

Ethical Basis: Retributive justice is grounded in the belief that wrongdoing deserves punishment and that justice is served when offenders receive their due. It focuses on the past actions of the offender and seeks to balance the scales of justice.

- Critiques: Critics of retributive justice argue that it can be overly punitive, fails to address the needs of victims, and may not contribute to the rehabilitation of offenders or the restoration of social harmony.

2. Utilitarianism

- Definition: Utilitarianism is a consequentialist theory of ethics that evaluates actions based on their outcomes. In the context of punishment, it seeks to impose penalties that maximize overall happiness and minimize suffering.

- Deterrence and Rehabilitation: Utilitarian theories of punishment emphasize deterrence (preventing future crimes by making an example of the offender) and rehabilitation (reforming the offender to prevent future wrongdoing). The focus is on the future consequences of punishment.

- Critiques: Utilitarian approaches can be criticized for justifying excessively harsh punishments if they are believed to deter crime effectively. They may also overlook the moral responsibility of the offender and the need for reparation to victims.

3. Restorative Justice

- Definition: Restorative justice is an approach to punishment that emphasizes repairing the harm caused by wrongdoing, involving all stakeholders in the justice process, and fostering reconciliation and healing.

- Ethical Basis: Restorative justice is grounded in the principles of relational ethics, communitarianism, and virtue ethics. It seeks to restore relationships, promote accountability, and address the needs of victims, offenders, and the community.

- Critiques: Some critics argue that restorative justice may be perceived as too lenient on offenders or that it may not be appropriate for all types of crimes. However, proponents contend that its focus on healing and accountability offers a more holistic and humane approach to justice.

Ethical Principles in Restorative Justice

Restorative justice is guided by several key ethical principles that shape its practices and objectives. These principles reflect its commitment to moral responsibility, community involvement, and the restoration of social harmony.

1. Accountability

- Moral Responsibility: Restorative justice emphasizes the importance of offenders taking moral responsibility for their actions. This involves acknowledging the harm caused, understanding its impact, and making amends.

- Active Participation: Offenders are encouraged to actively participate in the justice process, contributing to the development of solutions that promote healing and restoration.

2. Reparation

- Addressing Harm: A central tenet of restorative justice is the need to address the harm caused by wrongdoing. This involves providing restitution to victims, repairing damaged relationships, and restoring trust within the community.

- Collaborative Solutions: Restorative justice promotes collaborative problem-solving, where victims, offenders, and community members work together to find solutions that address the harm and promote healing.

3. Empathy and Compassion

- Fostering Understanding: Restorative justice seeks to foster empathy and compassion among all parties involved. This involves understanding the perspectives and experiences of others, acknowledging their pain, and working toward mutual healing.

- Healing Relationships: By promoting empathy and compassion, restorative justice aims to heal relationships and build stronger, more resilient communities.

4. Community Involvement

- Collective Responsibility: Restorative justice recognizes the role of the community in addressing crime and promoting justice. It involves community members in the justice process, emphasizing collective responsibility and the importance of social support.

- Building Trust: Community involvement in restorative justice helps build trust and solidarity, creating a sense of shared commitment to maintaining social harmony and preventing future harm.

5. Proportionality and Fairness

- Balanced Responses: Restorative justice seeks to ensure that responses to wrongdoing are proportional and fair, considering the severity of the offense, the needs of the victim, and the circumstances of the offender.

- Equity and Justice: By focusing on proportionality and fairness, restorative justice aims to achieve a more equitable and just outcome for all parties involved.

Ethical Challenges and Considerations

While restorative justice offers a compelling ethical framework, it also faces several challenges and considerations that must be addressed to ensure its effectiveness and integrity.

1. Balancing Accountability and Compassion

- Challenge: Finding the right balance between holding offenders accountable and showing compassion can be difficult. Ensuring that offenders take responsibility without feeling unfairly treated is crucial for the success of restorative justice.

- Consideration: Clear guidelines and practices are needed to maintain this balance, ensuring that accountability is meaningful and that compassion does not undermine the seriousness of the offense.

2. Ensuring Voluntary Participation

- Challenge: Restorative justice relies on the voluntary participation of victims, offenders, and community members. Coercion or lack of genuine engagement can undermine the process and its outcomes.

- Consideration: Measures must be taken to ensure that participation is truly voluntary and that all parties are fully informed and willing to engage in the restorative process.

3. Addressing Power Imbalances

- Challenge: Power imbalances between victims and offenders, or within the community, can affect the fairness and effectiveness of restorative justice practices. Ensuring that all voices are heard and respected is essential.

- Consideration: Facilitators must be trained to recognize and address power imbalances, creating a safe and equitable environment for all participants.

4. Cultural Sensitivity

- Challenge: Restorative justice practices must be culturally sensitive and appropriate for the communities in which they are implemented. A one-size-fits-all approach may not be effective or respectful of cultural differences.

- Consideration: Engaging with community leaders and members to adapt restorative practices to local cultural contexts is crucial for their success and acceptance.

Conclusion

Ethical considerations are central to the philosophy and practice of restorative justice. By emphasizing moral responsibility, reparation, empathy, community involvement, and fairness, restorative justice offers a humane and holistic approach to addressing harm and promoting justice. However, it also faces challenges that require careful consideration and ongoing reflection to ensure its effectiveness and integrity. Understanding these ethical foundations and challenges provides a deeper appreciation of the transformative potential of restorative justice and its role in creating more just and compassionate societies. In the chapters that follow, we will explore the core principles, practical applications, and real-world impact of restorative justice, building on the ethical considerations outlined in this chapter.

Restorative vs. Retributive Justice: Comparison of Restorative and Retributive Justice Models

The concepts of restorative and retributive justice represent two fundamentally different approaches to addressing crime and wrongdoing. While retributive justice focuses on punishment and retribution, restorative justice emphasizes healing, accountability, and the restoration of relationships. This chapter provides a detailed comparison of these two justice models, exploring their principles, processes, outcomes, and implications for individuals and communities.

Principles of Retributive Justice

Retributive justice is based on the principle that wrongdoing deserves punishment. It is a backward-looking approach that seeks to impose penalties proportionate to the offense, aiming to balance the scales of justice.

1. Just Deserts

- Moral Accountability: Retributive justice holds that offenders should receive their "just deserts," meaning that punishment should be proportional to the severity of the crime.

- Moral Order: This principle is rooted in the belief that maintaining a moral order requires that wrongdoing be met with appropriate consequences.

2. Deterrence

- Preventing Future Crimes: Retributive justice aims to deter future criminal behavior by making an example of the offender. The threat of punishment is intended to discourage both the individual offender and others from committing similar acts.

- General and Specific Deterrence: General deterrence targets the broader public, while specific deterrence focuses on preventing the individual offender from reoffending.

3. Retribution

- Punitive Response: Retributive justice views punishment as a necessary response to wrongdoing. It emphasizes the need for offenders to suffer consequences for their actions.

- Focus on Offender: The primary focus is on the offender and ensuring that they receive a penalty proportionate to their crime.

Principles of Restorative Justice

Restorative justice, in contrast, is a forward-looking approach that seeks to repair the harm caused by wrongdoing.

It involves all stakeholders in the justice process and aims to restore relationships and promote healing.

1. Repairing Harm

- Addressing Impact: Restorative justice focuses on addressing the harm caused by the offense, rather than simply punishing the offender. This includes the needs of victims, offenders, and the community.

- Making Amends: Offenders are encouraged to take responsibility for their actions and make amends to those harmed, often through restitution or other reparative actions.

2. Accountability

- Taking Responsibility: Restorative justice emphasizes the importance of offenders acknowledging their wrongdoing and understanding its impact on others.

- Active Participation: Offenders actively participate in the justice process, engaging with victims and the community to find solutions that promote healing and reconciliation.

3. Community Involvement

- Collective Responsibility: Restorative justice involves the community in the justice process, recognizing that crime affects not only the individuals directly involved but also the broader social fabric.

- Building Relationships: The goal is to rebuild trust and relationships within the community, fostering a sense of collective responsibility and support.

Processes in Retributive Justice

Retributive justice typically follows a formal, adversarial process within the legal system. Key elements include:

1. Adversarial System

- Prosecution and Defense: The legal process involves a contest between the prosecution and defense, each presenting their case to a judge or jury. The focus is on determining guilt and imposing punishment.

- Role of the State: The state acts as the primary party in prosecuting the offender, with the victim often playing a secondary role.

2. Focus on Guilt and Punishment

- Determining Guilt: The primary objective is to establish the guilt of the offender through evidence and legal arguments.

- Imposing Penalty: Once guilt is established, the court imposes a penalty proportional to the offense, often involving imprisonment, fines, or other forms of punishment.

3. Limited Victim Involvement

- Marginalized Role: In retributive justice, victims often have a limited role in the justice process. Their needs and perspectives may be secondary to the focus on punishment.

- Lack of Closure: This can result in victims feeling marginalized and unsatisfied with the justice process, as their emotional and practical needs may not be fully addressed.

Processes in Restorative Justice

Restorative justice involves a collaborative, inclusive process that engages all stakeholders. Key elements include:

1. Dialogue and Mediation

- Facilitated Meetings: Restorative justice processes often involve facilitated meetings between victims, offenders, and community members. These can take the form of victim-offender mediation, restorative circles, or family group conferences.

- Open Communication: The goal is to promote open communication, allowing all parties to share their perspectives, express their feelings, and work towards mutual understanding and resolution.

2. Focus on Healing and Reparation

- Addressing Needs: The process emphasizes addressing the needs of all stakeholders, including emotional healing for victims, accountability for offenders, and the restoration of community harmony.

- Reparative Actions: Offenders are encouraged to take concrete actions to make amends, such as providing restitution, performing community service, or engaging in other reparative activities.

3. Active Victim and Community Involvement

- Empowering Victims: Restorative justice empowers victims by giving them a central role in the justice process. They have the opportunity to express their needs, ask questions, and receive restitution.

- Community Engagement: Community members are involved in supporting victims, holding offenders accountable, and helping to find solutions that benefit the entire community.

Outcomes of Retributive Justice

Retributive justice outcomes are primarily focused on punishment and deterrence. Key outcomes include:

1. Punishment of Offender

- Penal Consequences: The offender receives a penalty proportionate to the offense, such as imprisonment, fines, or other forms of punishment.

- Moral Satisfaction: There is a sense of moral satisfaction in seeing the offender punished, which can reinforce social norms and the rule of law.

2. Deterrence

- General and Specific Deterrence: The punishment serves to deter the individual offender and others from committing similar crimes in the future.

- Focus on Consequences: The emphasis is on the consequences for the offender, rather than addressing the underlying causes of the behavior.

3. Potential Negative Outcomes

- High Recidivism Rates: Retributive justice often fails to address the root causes of criminal behavior, leading to high rates of recidivism.

- Victim Dissatisfaction: Victims may feel marginalized and unsatisfied with the justice process, as their needs for healing and restitution may not be fully addressed.

Outcomes of Restorative Justice

Restorative justice outcomes are focused on healing, accountability, and the restoration of relationships. Key outcomes include:

1. Healing and Reparation

- Addressing Harm: The primary focus is on addressing the harm caused by the offense, providing restitution to victims, and promoting emotional healing.

- Rebuilding Trust: Restorative justice aims to rebuild trust and relationships within the community, fostering a sense of collective responsibility and support.

2. Accountability and Rehabilitation

- Taking Responsibility: Offenders are encouraged to take responsibility for their actions, understand the impact of their behavior, and make amends.

- Personal Growth: The process promotes personal growth and rehabilitation, reducing the likelihood of reoffending and supporting the offender's reintegration into the community.

3. Positive Community Impact

- Strengthening Social Bonds: Restorative justice fosters stronger social bonds and a sense of collective responsibility. Communities become more resilient and better equipped to address conflicts and prevent crime.

- Building Trust: The inclusive and participatory nature of restorative justice helps build trust between community members, law enforcement, and the justice system.

Comparison of Models

The following table provides a summary comparison of the key elements of retributive and restorative justice models:

Aspect	Retributive Justice	Restorative Justice
Principles	Just Deserts, Deterrence, Retribution	Repairing Harm, Accountability, Community Involvement
Processes	Adversarial System, Focus on Guilt and Punishment	Dialogue and Mediation, Focus on Healing and Reparation
Victim Involvement	Limited	Central
Community Role	Marginalized	Active and Involved
Outcomes	Punishment, Deterrence, Potential Negative Outcomes	Healing, Reparation, Accountability, Positive Community Impact
Focus	Offender and Punishment	Victim, Offender, and Community

Conclusion

Restorative and retributive justice models represent two distinct approaches to addressing crime and wrongdoing. While retributive justice focuses on punishment and deterrence, restorative justice emphasizes healing, accountability, and the restoration of relationships. Understanding the principles, processes, and outcomes of these models provides valuable insights into their respective strengths and limitations. Restorative justice offers a holistic and humane approach to justice that addresses the needs of victims, offenders, and communities, promoting healing and social harmony. In the chapters that follow, we will explore the core principles, practical applications, and transformative potential of restorative justice, building on the theoretical frameworks outlined in this chapter.

CHAPTER 03

CORE PRINCIPLES AND VALUES

Accountability: The Role of Taking Responsibility in Restorative Justice

Accountability is a cornerstone of restorative justice, playing a critical role in the process of addressing harm and fostering healing. Unlike retributive justice, which focuses primarily on punishment, restorative justice emphasizes the importance of offenders taking responsibility for their actions, understanding the impact of their behavior, and making amends to those affected. This chapter explores the concept of accountability within restorative justice, its significance, and the ways in which it is facilitated through restorative practices.

Understanding Accountability in Restorative Justice

Accountability in restorative justice involves more than simply acknowledging guilt or accepting punishment. It encompasses a holistic understanding of the harm caused, taking responsibility for that harm, and actively participating in the process of making amends.

1. Acknowledging Harm

- Recognition of Impact: Offenders must recognize the full extent of the harm they have caused, including the emotional, psychological, and physical effects on victims and the community.

- Empathy and Understanding: Developing empathy for victims and understanding their experiences are crucial steps in the accountability process.

2. Taking Responsibility

- Ownership of Actions: Offenders are encouraged to take ownership of their actions and accept responsibility for the harm they have caused. This involves moving beyond excuses or justifications.

- Moral Accountability: Taking responsibility also involves recognizing the moral and ethical dimensions of one's actions and the violation of social and moral norms.

3. Making Amends

- Restitution and Reparation: Offenders are expected to take concrete actions to make amends for the harm caused. This may include financial restitution, community service, or other reparative actions.

- Active Participation: The process of making amends requires active participation from offenders, victims, and the community. It is a collaborative effort aimed at restoring relationships and promoting healing.

The Significance of Accountability in Restorative Justice

Accountability is significant in restorative justice for several reasons. It promotes personal growth, fosters healing, and contributes to the overall goal of restoring social harmony.

1. Promoting Personal Growth and Rehabilitation

- Self-Reflection: The process of taking responsibility encourages offenders to engage in self-reflection, examining the underlying causes of their behavior and the impact on others.

- Behavioral Change: By understanding the harm caused and taking steps to make amends, offenders are more likely to change their behavior and avoid future wrongdoing.

2. Fostering Healing for Victims

- Validation of Harm: When offenders acknowledge the harm they have caused, it validates the experiences and feelings of victims, contributing to their emotional and psychological healing.

- Restoring Trust: The process of making amends helps to rebuild trust between victims and offenders, as well as within the broader community.

3. Restoring Social Harmony

- Rebuilding Relationships: Accountability plays a crucial role in restoring relationships disrupted by crime. It helps to repair the social fabric and strengthen community bonds.

- Promoting Justice: By focusing on accountability and making amends, restorative justice promotes a more just and equitable resolution to conflicts and wrongdoing.

Facilitating Accountability through Restorative Practices

Restorative justice employs various practices to facilitate accountability, ensuring that offenders take responsibility for their actions and work towards making amends.

1. Victim-Offender Mediation

- Direct Dialogue: Victim-offender mediation provides a structured environment for direct dialogue between victims and offenders. This allows offenders to hear firsthand about the impact of their actions and to express remorse.

- Mutually Agreed Outcomes: Through mediation, victims and offenders work together to develop mutually agreed-upon outcomes that address the harm and promote healing.

2. Restorative Circles

- Inclusive Participation: Restorative circles involve victims, offenders, and community members in a collaborative process. Each participant has the opportunity to share their perspectives and contribute to the resolution.

- Collective Accountability: The circle process emphasizes collective accountability, encouraging offenders to take responsibility within the context of their community.

3. Family Group Conferencing

- Supportive Environment: Family group conferencing brings together the victim, offender, their families, and other supportive individuals. This approach provides a supportive environment for offenders to take responsibility and make amends.

- Family and Community Support: Involving family and community members helps to reinforce the accountability process and ensure that reparative actions are carried out.

4. Community Restorative Boards

- Community Involvement: Community restorative boards involve community members in the justice process, holding offenders accountable and supporting their efforts to make amends.

- Restorative Agreements: These boards often develop restorative agreements that outline specific actions offenders will take to address the harm and contribute positively to the community.

Challenges and Considerations in Promoting Accountability

While accountability is a core principle of restorative justice, promoting it effectively involves several challenges and considerations.

1. Ensuring Genuine Accountability

- Voluntary Participation: For accountability to be meaningful, participation in restorative processes must be voluntary. Coercion or pressure can undermine the sincerity of the offender's acceptance of responsibility.

- Authentic Engagement: Facilitators must ensure that offenders are genuinely engaged in the process and that their expressions of remorse and commitment to making amends are authentic.

2. Addressing Power Imbalances

- Equitable Participation: Power imbalances between victims and offenders, or within the community, can affect the fairness and effectiveness of restorative processes. Facilitators must work to create a safe and equitable environment for all participants.

- Support and Advocacy: Providing support and advocacy for victims and offenders can help address power imbalances and ensure that all voices are heard and respected.

3. Measuring Accountability

- Defining Success: Measuring the success of accountability in restorative justice can be challenging. Success may be defined not only by the completion of reparative actions but also by the personal growth of the offender and the healing of the victim and community.

- Ongoing Monitoring: Ongoing monitoring and support are often necessary to ensure that offenders follow through on their commitments and that the intended outcomes are achieved.

Conclusion

Accountability is a fundamental principle of restorative justice, playing a crucial role in addressing harm, promoting healing, and restoring social harmony. By encouraging offenders to take responsibility for their actions, understand the impact of their behavior, and actively participate in making amends, restorative justice fosters personal growth, victim healing, and community resilience. While promoting accountability presents challenges, the collaborative and inclusive nature of restorative practices helps to ensure that the process is meaningful and effective. In the chapters that follow, we will continue to explore the core principles and values of restorative justice, delving into the roles of reparation, community involvement, empathy, and healing in creating a more just and compassionate society.

Reparation: Making Amends and Repairing Harm

Reparation is a central tenet of restorative justice, focusing on addressing and repairing the harm caused by wrongdoing. Unlike retributive justice, which prioritizes punishment, restorative justice seeks to restore balance by ensuring that offenders take meaningful actions to make amends to those they have harmed. This chapter delves into the concept of reparation, its significance, and the various ways it is facilitated within restorative justice practices.

Understanding Reparation in Restorative Justice

Reparation in restorative justice goes beyond compensation; it involves a holistic approach to addressing harm and promoting healing. It requires offenders to acknowledge the impact of their actions and take active steps to restore the well-being of victims and the community.

1. Acknowledging Harm

- Recognition of Impact: Offenders must understand the full extent of the harm they have caused, including physical, emotional, psychological, and social dimensions.

- Empathy and Responsibility: Developing empathy for victims and accepting responsibility for the harm are crucial steps in the reparation process.

2. Making Amends

- Concrete Actions: Reparation involves taking specific actions to address the harm. This can include financial restitution, community service, or direct apologies.

- Symbolic Acts: In addition to tangible actions, symbolic acts of contrition and reconciliation play a vital role in the healing process.

3. Promoting Healing

- Restoring Relationships: Reparation aims to repair relationships disrupted by wrongdoing, fostering trust and understanding between victims, offenders, and the community.

- Holistic Healing: The goal is to promote holistic healing, addressing not just the immediate harm but also the broader implications for individuals and communities.

The Significance of Reparation in Restorative Justice

Reparation is significant in restorative justice for several reasons. It addresses the needs of victims, promotes offender rehabilitation, and contributes to the restoration of social harmony.

1. Addressing Victims' Needs

- Validation and Empowerment: Reparation validates the experiences and feelings of victims, providing a sense of justice and empowerment.

- Material and Emotional Support: It ensures that victims receive both material restitution and emotional support, facilitating their recovery and well-being.

2. Promoting Offender Rehabilitation

- Accountability and Growth: The process of making amends encourages offenders to take accountability for their actions, fostering personal growth and moral development.

- Reintegration: Reparation supports the reintegration of offenders into the community by demonstrating their commitment to positive change and responsible behavior.

3. Restoring Social Harmony

- Rebuilding Trust: Reparation helps rebuild trust within the community, promoting social cohesion and mutual support.

- Preventing Recurrence: By addressing the root causes of harm and promoting accountability, reparation contributes to the prevention of future wrongdoing.

Facilitating Reparation through Restorative Practices

Restorative justice employs various practices to facilitate reparation, ensuring that offenders take meaningful actions to address the harm and promote healing.

1. Victim-Offender Mediation

- Direct Dialogue: Victim-offender mediation provides a structured environment for direct dialogue between victims and offenders. This allows offenders to understand the impact of their actions and to agree on ways to make amends.

- Mutually Agreed Outcomes: Through mediation, victims and offenders work together to develop mutually agreed-upon outcomes that address the harm and promote healing.

2. Restorative Circles

- Inclusive Participation: Restorative circles involve victims, offenders, and community members in a collaborative process. Each participant has the opportunity to share their perspectives and contribute to the resolution.

- Collective Reparation: The circle process emphasizes collective reparation, encouraging offenders to make amends within the context of their community.

3. Family Group Conferencing

- Supportive Environment: Family group conferencing brings together the victim, offender, their families, and other supportive individuals. This approach provides a supportive environment for offenders to take responsibility and make amends.

- Family and Community Support: Involving family and community members helps to reinforce the reparation process and ensure that reparative actions are carried out.

4. Community Restorative Boards

- Community Involvement: Community restorative boards involve community members in the justice process, holding offenders accountable and supporting their efforts to make amends.

- Restorative Agreements: These boards often develop restorative agreements that outline specific actions offenders will take to address the harm and contribute positively to the community.

Types of Reparation

Reparation in restorative justice can take various forms, each tailored to address different aspects of harm and promote healing.

1. Financial Restitution

- Compensation for Losses: Offenders provide financial compensation to victims to cover medical expenses, property damage, or other financial losses resulting from the offense.

- Symbolic Value: While monetary compensation cannot undo the harm, it serves as a tangible acknowledgment of responsibility and an effort to make amends.

2. Community Service

- Giving Back: Offenders engage in community service projects that benefit the community, demonstrating their commitment to making amends and contributing positively to society.

- Restoring Community Trust: Community service helps to restore trust between offenders and the community, facilitating their reintegration.

3. Direct Apologies and Reconciliation

- Personal Apologies: Offenders offer direct apologies to victims, expressing remorse and taking responsibility for their actions.

- Reconciliation Efforts: Efforts to reconcile with victims and the community, such as participating in restorative circles or other reparative activities, promote healing and restore relationships.

4. Symbolic Acts

- Rituals and Ceremonies: Symbolic acts, such as public apologies or participation in reconciliation ceremonies, play a significant role in acknowledging harm and promoting healing.

- Restoring Social Harmony: These acts reinforce the offender's commitment to making amends and restoring social harmony.

Challenges and Considerations in Promoting Reparation

While reparation is a core principle of restorative justice, promoting it effectively involves several challenges and considerations.

1. Ensuring Meaningful Reparation

- Voluntary Participation: For reparation to be meaningful, participation in restorative processes must be voluntary. Coercion or pressure can undermine the sincerity of the offender's reparative actions.

- Authentic Engagement: Facilitators must ensure that offenders are genuinely engaged in the process and that their reparative actions are sincere and meaningful.

2. Addressing Power Imbalances

- Equitable Participation: Power imbalances between victims and offenders, or within the community, can affect the fairness and effectiveness of restorative processes. Facilitators must work to create a safe and equitable environment for all participants.

- Support and Advocacy: Providing support and advocacy for victims and offenders can help address power imbalances and ensure that all voices are heard and respected.

3. Measuring Reparation

- Defining Success: Measuring the success of reparation in restorative justice can be challenging. Success may be defined not only by the completion of reparative actions but also by the personal growth of the offender and the healing of the victim and community.

- Ongoing Monitoring: Ongoing monitoring and support are often necessary to ensure that offenders follow through on their commitments and that the intended outcomes are achieved.

Conclusion

Reparation is a fundamental principle of restorative justice, playing a crucial role in addressing harm, promoting healing, and restoring social harmony. By encouraging offenders to take responsibility for their actions, understand the impact of their behavior, and actively participate in making amends, restorative justice fosters personal growth, victim healing, and community resilience. While promoting reparation presents challenges, the collaborative and inclusive nature of restorative practices helps to ensure that the process is meaningful and effective. In the chapters that follow, we will continue to explore the core principles and values of restorative justice, delving into the roles of community involvement, empathy, and healing in creating a more just and compassionate society.

Community Involvement: The Significance of Community Participation in the Justice Process

Community involvement is a central pillar of restorative justice, emphasizing the importance of engaging the community in the justice process. This approach recognizes that crime affects not only the direct victims but also the broader community, and that the community has a vital role to play in addressing harm, supporting victims, and promoting offender accountability. This chapter explores the significance of community participation in restorative justice, its benefits, and the various ways it is facilitated through restorative practices.

Understanding Community Involvement in Restorative Justice

Community involvement in restorative justice involves actively engaging community members in the justice process to address harm, support victims, and hold offenders accountable. It is based on the belief that the community is a key stakeholder in maintaining social harmony and justice.

1. Community as Stakeholders

- Collective Responsibility: The community is seen as collectively responsible for maintaining social order and supporting the justice process.

- Impact of Crime: Recognizing that crime impacts the entire community, not just the direct victim and offender, emphasizes the need for a collective response.

2. Roles of Community Members

- Support for Victims: Community members provide emotional, social, and practical support to victims, helping them recover and feel safe.

- Accountability for Offenders: The community holds offenders accountable, supporting their efforts to make amends and reintegrate into society.

- Facilitation and Mediation: Trained community members often serve as facilitators or mediators in restorative processes, guiding dialogues and ensuring a fair and respectful process.

The Significance of Community Participation

Community participation in restorative justice is significant for several reasons. It enhances the justice process, promotes healing, and strengthens social cohesion.

1. Enhancing the Justice Process

- Inclusive Decision-Making: Involving the community in the justice process ensures that decisions reflect the values and needs of the broader society, leading to more holistic and inclusive outcomes.

- Shared Responsibility: Community involvement promotes a sense of shared responsibility for addressing harm and maintaining social order, reducing the burden on the formal justice system.

2. Promoting Healing and Support

- Support Networks: Community members provide vital support networks for victims, offering practical assistance, emotional comfort, and a sense of belonging.

- Restorative Healing: Community participation fosters a supportive environment for offenders to take responsibility, make amends, and rehabilitate, promoting restorative healing for all parties involved.

3. Strengthening Social Cohesion

- Building Trust: Engaging the community in the justice process helps build trust between community members, victims, offenders, and the justice system.

- Resilient Communities: Community involvement strengthens social bonds and resilience, creating a collective commitment to preventing future harm and promoting a culture of care and mutual support.

Facilitating Community Involvement through Restorative Practices

Restorative justice employs various practices to facilitate community involvement, ensuring that community members play an active role in addressing harm and promoting justice.

1. Restorative Circles

- Inclusive Participation: Restorative circles involve victims, offenders, and community members in a collaborative process. Each participant has the opportunity to share their perspectives and contribute to the resolution.

- Collective Decision-Making: The circle process emphasizes collective decision-making, where the community helps develop and support reparative actions.

2. Family Group Conferencing

\- Supportive Environment: Family group conferencing brings together the victim, offender, their families, and other supportive individuals. This approach provides a supportive environment for addressing harm and making amends.

- Family and Community Support: Involving family and community members reinforces the accountability process and ensures that reparative actions are carried out effectively.

3. Community Restorative Boards

- Community Involvement: Community restorative boards involve community members in the justice process, holding offenders accountable and supporting their efforts to make amends.

- Restorative Agreements: These boards often develop restorative agreements that outline specific actions offenders will take to address the harm and contribute positively to the community.

4. Victim-offender mediation with Community Support

- Support Systems: Victim-offender mediation sessions can include community support persons who provide additional perspectives and support for both victims and offenders.

- Community-Endorsed Solutions: The involvement of community members helps ensure that the solutions developed are endorsed and supported by the broader community.

Benefits of Community Involvement

Community involvement in restorative justice offers numerous benefits for victims, offenders, and the community as a whole.

1. For Victims

- Enhanced Support: Victims receive broader support from their community, helping them recover and feel validated in their experiences.

- Greater Satisfaction: Victims often report higher levels of satisfaction with the justice process when it involves their community, as it addresses their needs more comprehensively.

2. For Offenders

- Reintegration Support: Community involvement provides a support system for offenders, aiding their reintegration and promoting positive behavioral change.

- Accountability: Offenders are held accountable not only to their victims but also to their community, reinforcing the importance of making amends and contributing positively to society.

3. For the Community

- Strengthened Social Bonds: Community participation in the justice process strengthens social bonds and fosters a sense of collective responsibility and mutual support.

- Increased Trust in the Justice System: When the community is actively involved in the justice process, trust in the justice system is enhanced, promoting greater cooperation and engagement in future initiatives.

Challenges and Considerations in Promoting Community Involvement

While community involvement is a core principle of restorative justice, promoting it effectively involves several challenges and considerations.

1. Ensuring Meaningful Participation

- Voluntary Engagement: For community involvement to be meaningful, participation must be voluntary and based on genuine interest and commitment.

- Inclusivity: Efforts must be made to ensure that all voices in the community are heard and respected, including marginalized or underrepresented groups.

2. Addressing Power Imbalances

- Equitable Participation: Power imbalances within the community can affect the fairness and effectiveness of restorative processes. Facilitators must work to create a safe and equitable environment for all participants.

- Support and Advocacy: Providing support and advocacy for vulnerable community members can help address power imbalances and ensure that their perspectives are considered.

3. Sustaining Community Engagement

- Ongoing Involvement: Sustaining community engagement requires ongoing efforts to build trust, foster relationships, and maintain a sense of collective responsibility.

- Capacity Building: Investing in community capacity building, such as training and resources, can enhance the community's ability to participate effectively in the justice process.

Conclusion

Community involvement is a fundamental principle of restorative justice, playing a crucial role in addressing harm, promoting healing, and restoring social harmony. By engaging community members in the justice process, restorative justice fosters a sense of collective responsibility, support, and mutual accountability. While promoting community involvement presents challenges, the collaborative and inclusive nature of restorative practices helps to ensure that the process is meaningful and effective. In the chapters that follow, we will continue to explore the core principles and values of restorative justice, delving into the roles of empathy, healing, and other essential components in creating a more just and compassionate society.

Empathy and Healing: Fostering Empathy and Emotional Healing

Empathy and healing are integral components of restorative justice, emphasizing the importance of understanding, compassion, and emotional recovery. By fostering empathy and facilitating healing, restorative justice seeks to repair the emotional and psychological harm caused by wrongdoing, promoting reconciliation and restoring social harmony. This chapter explores the role of empathy and healing in restorative justice, their significance, and the ways in which they are cultivated through restorative practices.

Understanding Empathy in Restorative Justice

Empathy, the ability to understand and share the feelings of others, is crucial in restorative justice. It enables offenders to recognize the impact of their actions, and it helps victims feel heard and validated.

1. Defining Empathy

- Cognitive Empathy: The intellectual understanding of another person's feelings and perspectives.

- Emotional Empathy: The capacity to feel what another person is experiencing emotionally.

- Compassionate Empathy: The desire to help and support others based on understanding and sharing their feelings.

2. The Role of Empathy in Restorative Justice

- Building Understanding: Empathy helps offenders understand the impact of their actions on victims, fostering a sense of responsibility and remorse.

- Promoting Reconciliation: Empathy facilitates reconciliation by helping victims and offenders connect on a human level, breaking down barriers of anger and resentment.

- Enhancing Healing: Empathy promotes healing by validating the emotions and experiences of victims, providing them with the emotional support needed to recover.

The Significance of Healing in Restorative Justice

Healing is a central goal of restorative justice, addressing the emotional and psychological wounds caused by wrongdoing. It involves not only the victims and offenders but also the broader community.

1. Types of Healing

Emotional Healing: Addressing the emotional pain and trauma experienced by victims and offenders.

- Psychological Healing: Promoting mental well-being and resilience in the aftermath of harm.

- Social Healing: Restoring trust and harmony within the community, rebuilding social bonds.

2. The Role of Healing in Restorative Justice

- Restoring Well-Being: Healing processes aim to restore the well-being of victims, helping them move beyond the trauma and regain a sense of security and peace.

- Rehabilitating Offenders: Healing also involves the rehabilitation of offenders, addressing underlying issues and promoting positive behavioral change.

- Rebuilding Communities: By fostering healing, restorative justice helps rebuild trust and cohesion within the community, promoting long-term resilience and harmony.

Facilitating Empathy and Healing through Restorative Practices

Restorative justice employs various practices to facilitate empathy and promote healing, ensuring that all parties involved can move forward positively.

1. Victim-Offender Mediation

- Direct Dialogue: Mediation provides a structured environment for direct dialogue between victims and offenders, allowing for the expression of feelings and the development of mutual understanding.

- Emotional Expression: Both parties can openly share their emotions, fostering empathy and facilitating emotional healing.

2. Restorative Circles

- Inclusive Participation: Restorative circles involve victims, offenders, and community members in a collaborative process, promoting open communication and empathy.

- Shared Experiences: Participants share their experiences and feelings, creating a supportive environment for emotional healing and mutual understanding.

3. Family Group Conferencing

- Supportive Environment: Family group conferencing brings together the victim, offender, their families, and other supportive individuals, providing a safe space for expressing emotions and fostering empathy.

- Collective Healing: The involvement of family and community members enhances the healing process, offering broader emotional support and understanding.

4. Community Restorative Boards

- Community Involvement: Community restorative boards involve community members in the justice process, providing additional perspectives and support for empathy and healing.

- Restorative Agreements: These boards often develop restorative agreements that include actions to promote healing, such as counseling or community service.

Strategies for Fostering Empathy and Healing

Several strategies can be employed to foster empathy and promote healing within restorative justice processes.

1. Active Listening

- Creating Safe Spaces: Facilitators create safe spaces for participants to share their feelings without fear of judgment or retaliation.

- Validation: Active listening involves validating the emotions and experiences of all parties, reinforcing the importance of their perspectives.

2. Narrative Sharing

- Personal Stories: Encouraging participants to share their personal stories helps build empathy and understanding, highlighting the human impact of wrongdoing.

- Mutual Recognition: Narrative sharing promotes mutual recognition of pain and suffering, fostering a sense of shared humanity and compassion.

3. Emotional Support

- Counseling and Therapy: Providing access to counseling and therapeutic support helps victims and offenders process their emotions and begin the healing journey.

- Peer Support: Peer support groups offer a sense of community and understanding, helping participants feel less isolated in their experiences.

4. Reparative Actions

- Symbolic Acts: Symbolic acts of contrition, such as public apologies or participation in reconciliation ceremonies, play a significant role in acknowledging harm and promoting healing.

- Concrete Actions: Reparative actions, such as financial restitution or community service, demonstrate a commitment to making amends and contribute to the healing process.

Benefits of Empathy and Healing in Restorative Justice

Fostering empathy and promoting healing offer numerous benefits for victims, offenders, and the community as a whole.

1. For Victims

- Emotional Validation: Empathy and healing provide emotional validation, helping victims feel heard, understood, and supported.

- Recovery and Resilience: The healing process promotes recovery and resilience, enabling victims to rebuild their lives and move forward positively.

2. For Offenders

- Moral Growth: Empathy fosters moral growth and personal development, encouraging offenders to take responsibility and make positive changes.

- Rehabilitation: Healing processes support the rehabilitation of offenders, addressing underlying issues and reducing the likelihood of reoffending.

3. For the Community

- Strengthened Social Bonds: Empathy and healing strengthen social bonds, fostering a sense of collective responsibility and mutual support.

- Increased Trust: Community involvement in the healing process builds trust and cooperation, promoting a more cohesive and resilient community.

Challenges and Considerations in Fostering Empathy and Healing

While empathy and healing are core principles of restorative justice, promoting them effectively involves several challenges and considerations.

1. Ensuring Genuine Empathy

- Voluntary Participation: For empathy to be genuine, participation in restorative processes must be voluntary and based on genuine interest and commitment.

- Authentic Engagement: Facilitators must ensure that participants are genuinely engaged in the process and that their expressions of empathy and commitment to healing are sincere.

2. Addressing Emotional Barriers

- Emotional Resistance: Participants may have emotional barriers that hinder their ability to empathize or heal. Facilitators must be skilled in addressing and overcoming these barriers.

- Support and Counseling: Providing access to support and counseling can help participants process their emotions and engage more fully in the empathy and healing process.

3. Creating Safe Spaces

- Safe Environment: Creating a safe and supportive environment is crucial for fostering empathy and healing.

Participants must feel secure and respected throughout the process.

- Confidentiality and Trust: Maintaining confidentiality and building trust are essential for creating an environment where participants feel comfortable expressing their emotions.

Conclusion

Empathy and healing are fundamental principles of restorative justice, playing a crucial role in addressing harm, promoting understanding, and restoring social harmony. By fostering empathy and facilitating healing, restorative justice helps repair the emotional and psychological wounds caused by wrongdoing, promoting reconciliation and building stronger, more resilient communities. While promoting empathy and healing presents challenges, the collaborative and inclusive nature of restorative practices helps ensure that the process is meaningful and effective. In the chapters that follow, we will continue to explore the core principles and values of restorative justice, delving into the roles of accountability, community involvement, and other essential components in creating a more just and compassionate society.

CHAPTER 04

RESTORATIVE PRACTICES AND MODELS

Victim-Offender Mediation: The Process and Benefits of Direct Mediation

Victim-offender mediation (VOM) is a restorative justice practice that brings victims and offenders together in a facilitated dialogue to address the harm caused by a crime. This chapter explores the process of victim-offender mediation, its benefits for both victims and offenders, and its broader impact on the community and justice system.

Understanding Victim-Offender Mediation

Victim-offender mediation is a structured process that provides a safe and supportive environment for victims and offenders to communicate directly. The goal is to promote understanding, accountability, and healing through a facilitated dialogue.

1. Definition of Victim-Offender Mediation

- Direct Dialogue: VOM involves face-to-face meetings between victims and offenders, facilitated by a trained mediator.

- Restorative Goals: The primary goals are to address the harm caused, promote accountability, and facilitate healing for both parties.

2. Key Principles of Victim-Offender Mediation

- Voluntary Participation: Participation in VOM is voluntary for both victims and offenders. Both parties must agree to engage in the process willingly.

- Confidentiality: The mediation process is confidential, ensuring that participants can speak openly and honestly without fear of repercussions.

- Neutral Facilitation: A trained mediator facilitates the dialogue, ensuring a balanced and respectful conversation.

The Process of Victim-Offender Mediation

The VOM process involves several stages, each designed to promote effective communication, understanding, and resolution.

1. Referral and Intake

- Case Referral: Cases can be referred to VOM by the justice system, community organizations, or through self-referral by the parties involved.

- Intake Assessment: Mediators conduct an intake assessment to determine the suitability of the case for mediation. They evaluate the willingness of both parties to participate and assess any potential risks or safety concerns.

2. Preparation

- Pre-Mediation Meetings: Mediators meet separately with victims and offenders to prepare them for the mediation session. These meetings help build trust, explain the process, and address any concerns.

- Setting Ground Rules: Mediators establish ground rules for the mediation session, ensuring that both parties understand and agree to the guidelines for respectful communication.

3. Mediation Session

- Facilitated Dialogue: During the mediation session, the mediator facilitates a structured dialogue between the victim and offender. The mediator guides the conversation, ensuring that both parties have an opportunity to speak and be heard.

- Exploring Impact: The dialogue focuses on exploring the impact of the crime, allowing the victim to express their feelings and the offender to understand the consequences of their actions.

- Developing Agreements: The session may result in a mutually agreed-upon plan for reparation, which can include actions such as apologies, restitution, community service, or other forms of making amends.

4. Follow-Up

- Monitoring Agreements: Mediators may follow up with both parties to ensure that the agreed-upon actions are carried out and to provide ongoing support if needed.

- Additional Sessions: If necessary, additional mediation sessions can be arranged to address unresolved issues or further support the healing process.

Benefits of Victim-Offender Mediation

Victim-offender mediation offers numerous benefits for victims, offenders, and the broader community. It promotes healing, accountability, and the restoration of relationships.

1. Benefits for Victims

- Empowerment: VOM empowers victims by giving them a voice in the justice process and an opportunity to express their feelings and needs directly to the offender.

- Emotional Healing: The process provides a platform for victims to confront the offender, ask questions, and receive answers, facilitating emotional healing and closure.

- Restitution and Reparation: Victims have the opportunity to negotiate restitution and reparation, addressing their material and emotional needs.

2. Benefits for Offenders

- Accountability: VOM encourages offenders to take responsibility for their actions and understand the impact of their behavior on the victim and community.

- Personal Growth: The process promotes personal growth and rehabilitation, helping offenders to develop empathy, remorse, and a commitment to making amends.

- Reduced Recidivism: Research indicates that participation in VOM can reduce recidivism rates, as offenders are more likely to change their behavior when they understand the harm they have caused and feel a sense of accountability.

3. Benefits for the Community

- Restoring Social Harmony: VOM helps restore social harmony by addressing the underlying harm caused by crime and promoting reconciliation between victims and offenders.

- Community Involvement: The process fosters community involvement in the justice process, reinforcing collective responsibility and support for both victims and offenders.

- Alternative to Traditional Justice: VOM provides an alternative to the traditional justice system, offering a more humane and restorative approach to addressing crime.

Case Studies and Examples

Examining real-life examples of victim-offender mediation highlights the effectiveness and impact of the process in various contexts.

1. Juvenile Offenders

- Case Study: In a case involving a juvenile offender who vandalized a local park, VOM was used to facilitate a dialogue between the offender and the community members affected by the vandalism.

- Outcome: The offender expressed remorse, agreed to participate in community service to repair the damage, and developed a deeper understanding of the impact of their actions. The community members felt heard and supported the offender's rehabilitation.

2. Property Crimes

- Case Study: In a case of burglary, the victim and offender participated in VOM to address the emotional and material harm caused by the crime.

- Outcome: The offender apologized and agreed to provide restitution for the stolen items. The victim gained a sense of closure and felt safer knowing that the offender understood the impact of their actions.

3. Violent Crimes

- Case Study: In a case involving an assault, VOM facilitated a dialogue between the victim and offender to address the physical and emotional harm caused.

- Outcome: The offender expressed deep remorse and agreed to participate in anger management counseling. The victim felt empowered by the opportunity to confront the offender and received support for their healing process.

Challenges and Considerations in Victim-Offender Mediation

While VOM offers significant benefits, it also presents several challenges and considerations that must be addressed to ensure its effectiveness and fairness.

1. Ensuring Voluntary Participation

- Genuine Consent: For VOM to be effective, participation must be truly voluntary. Coercion or pressure to participate can undermine the sincerity and outcomes of the mediation process.

- Informed Decision-Making: Both victims and offenders must be fully informed about the process and its potential outcomes before agreeing to participate.

2. Addressing Power Imbalances

- Equitable Participation: Power imbalances between victims and offenders can affect the fairness and effectiveness of the mediation. Mediators must be skilled in addressing and mitigating these imbalances to ensure a balanced dialogue.

- Support and Advocacy: Providing support and advocacy for vulnerable participants can help address power imbalances and ensure that all voices are heard and respected.

3. Safety and Emotional Well-Being

- Creating a Safe Environment: Ensuring the physical and emotional safety of all participants is paramount. Mediators must create a safe and respectful environment for the dialogue.

- Emotional Support: Providing access to emotional support and counseling for both victims and offenders can help them process their feelings and engage more fully in the mediation.

4. Cultural Sensitivity

- Respecting Diversity: VOM must be culturally sensitive and appropriate for the participants involved.

Mediators should be trained to understand and respect cultural differences and adapt the process accordingly.

- Community Engagement: Engaging with community leaders and members can help ensure that the mediation process is respectful of and responsive to cultural norms and values.

Conclusion

Victim-offender mediation is a powerful restorative justice practice that promotes healing, accountability, and the restoration of relationships. By facilitating direct dialogue between victims and offenders, VOM addresses the harm caused by crime, empowers victims, supports offender rehabilitation, and fosters community involvement. While promoting VOM presents challenges, the collaborative and inclusive nature of the process helps ensure that it is meaningful and effective. In the chapters that follow, we will continue to explore various restorative practices and models, delving into their principles, processes, and impacts in creating a more just and compassionate society.

Family Group Conferencing: Involving Family and Community in the Resolution Process

Family Group Conferencing (FGC) is a restorative justice practice that involves the victim, offender, their families, and community members in the process of resolving harm and restoring relationships. This chapter explores the principles, process, and benefits of Family Group Conferencing, as well as its impact on individuals and communities.

Understanding Family Group Conferencing

Family Group Conferencing is based on the belief that families and communities play a crucial role in addressing harm and supporting the rehabilitation of offenders. It emphasizes collective responsibility and collaborative decision-making.

1. Definition of Family Group Conferencing

- Inclusive Process: FGC brings together victims, offenders, their families, and other supportive community members in a structured meeting to discuss the harm caused and to develop a plan for making amends.

- Restorative Goals: The primary goals are to address the harm, promote accountability, and foster healing for all parties involved.

2. Key Principles of Family Group Conferencing

- Family and Community Involvement: FGC recognizes the importance of involving the offender's family and the broader community in the justice process.

- Collective Decision-Making: Decisions are made collaboratively, with input from all participants, ensuring that the outcomes are fair and supported by those involved.

- Empowerment: FGC empowers families and communities to take an active role in resolving harm and supporting the offender's rehabilitation.

The Process of Family Group Conferencing

The FGC process involves several stages, each designed to facilitate effective communication, mutual understanding, and collaborative resolution.

1. Referral and Preparation

- Case Referral: Cases can be referred to FGC by the justice system, social services, or community organizations. The suitability of the case for FGC is assessed, considering the willingness of the parties to participate.

- Preparation Meetings: Facilitators meet separately with the victim, offender, and their families to explain the process, address any concerns, and prepare them for the conference.

2. The Conference

- Opening: The conference begins with an introduction by the facilitator, who outlines the purpose and ground rules for the meeting.

- Sharing Stories: Participants share their stories, with the victim describing the impact of the harm and the offender acknowledging their actions. Family and community members provide support and offer their perspectives.

- Private Family Time: Families and supporters have a private discussion to develop a plan for making amends, addressing the needs of the victim, and supporting the offender's rehabilitation.

- Agreement Development: The conference reconvenes to discuss and finalize the plan, ensuring that it is fair and achievable. All participants must agree on the proposed actions.

3. Follow-Up

- Monitoring Implementation: Facilitators and community members monitor the implementation of the agreed-upon plan, providing support and addressing any challenges that arise.

- Additional Meetings: Follow-up meetings may be held to review progress, make adjustments to the plan if necessary, and ensure that the outcomes are being achieved.

Benefits of Family Group Conferencing

Family Group Conferencing offers numerous benefits for victims, offenders, and the broader community. It promotes healing, accountability, and social cohesion.

1. Benefits for Victims

- Empowerment and Voice: FGC provides victims with an opportunity to express their feelings, ask questions, and have a say in the resolution process.

- Emotional Healing: The supportive environment and acknowledgment of harm by the offender contribute to the victim's emotional healing and sense of justice.

- Restitution and Support: Victims receive tangible restitution and support from the offender's family and community, addressing their material and emotional needs.

2. Benefits for Offenders

- Accountability and Responsibility: FGC encourages offenders to take responsibility for their actions, understand the impact of their behavior and make amends.

- Supportive Environment: The involvement of family and community provides a supportive environment for the offender's rehabilitation and reintegration.

- Personal Growth: The process promotes personal growth, empathy, and positive behavioral change, reducing the likelihood of reoffending.

3. Benefits for the Community

- Strengthened Relationships: FGC fosters stronger relationships within families and communities, promoting mutual support and collective responsibility.

- Social Harmony: The process helps restore social harmony by addressing the underlying harm and promoting reconciliation between victims, offenders, and the community.

- Alternative to Traditional Justice: FGC provides an alternative to the traditional justice system, offering a more restorative and community-based approach to addressing harm.

Case Studies and Examples

Examining real-life examples of Family Group Conferencing highlights the effectiveness and impact of the process in various contexts.

1. Youth Offenses

- Case Study: In a case involving a teenager who committed vandalism, FGC was used to bring together the victim, the offender, and their families.

- Outcome: The teenager expressed remorse, agreed to repair the damage, and participated in community service. The victim felt heard and supported, and the families developed a plan to support the teenager's positive behavior.

2. Domestic Disputes

- Case Study: In a case of a domestic dispute, FGC facilitated a dialogue between the family members involved, including the victim, offender, and their extended family.

- Outcome: The offender took responsibility for their actions, and the family developed a plan for counseling and support. The victim felt empowered, and the family committed to creating a safer home environment.

3. School-Based Incidents

- Case Study: In a school setting, FGC addressed a bullying incident by bringing together the victim, offender, their families, and school staff.

- Outcome: The offender apologized and agreed to participate in a peer mentoring program. The victims received support from their peers and teachers, and the school community worked together to create a more inclusive environment.

Challenges and Considerations in Family Group Conferencing

While FGC offers significant benefits, it also presents several challenges and considerations that must be addressed to ensure its effectiveness and fairness.

1. Ensuring Voluntary Participation

- Genuine Consent: For FGC to be effective, participation must be truly voluntary. Coercion or pressure to participate can undermine the sincerity and outcomes of the conference.

- Informed Decision-Making: Both victims and offenders, along with their families, must be fully informed about the process and its potential outcomes before agreeing to participate.

2. Addressing Power Imbalances

- Equitable Participation: Power imbalances between victims and offenders, or within the family, can affect the fairness and effectiveness of the conference. Facilitators must be skilled in addressing and mitigating these imbalances to ensure a balanced dialogue.

- Support and Advocacy: Providing support and advocacy for vulnerable participants can help address power imbalances and ensure that all voices are heard and respected.

3. Creating a Safe Environment

- Safety Concerns: Ensuring the physical and emotional safety of all participants is paramount. Facilitators must create a safe and respectful environment for the dialogue.

- Emotional Support: Providing access to emotional support and counseling for both victims and offenders can help them process their feelings and engage more fully in the conference.

4. Cultural Sensitivity

- Respecting Diversity: FGC must be culturally sensitive and appropriate for the participants involved. Facilitators should be trained to understand and respect cultural differences and adapt the process accordingly.

- Community Engagement: Engaging with community leaders and members can help ensure that the conference process is respectful of and responsive to cultural norms and values.

Conclusion

Family Group Conferencing is a powerful restorative justice practice that promotes healing, accountability, and the restoration of relationships. By involving families and communities in the resolution process, FGC addresses the harm caused by wrongdoing, empowers victims, supports offender rehabilitation, and fosters social cohesion. While promoting FGC presents challenges, the collaborative and inclusive nature of the process helps ensure that it is meaningful and effective. In the chapters that follow, we will continue to explore various restorative practices and models, delving into their principles, processes, and impacts in creating a more just and compassionate society.

Circle Processes: The Role of Restorative Circles in Conflict Resolution

Circle processes, also known as restorative circles, are a fundamental component of restorative justice practices. These processes involve bringing together victims, offenders, and community members in a structured, inclusive environment to address harm, promote healing, and resolve conflicts. This chapter explores the principles, process, and benefits of circle processes, as well as their broader impact on individuals and communities.

Understanding Circle Processes

Restorative circles are based on indigenous practices that emphasize community, dialogue, and collective responsibility. They are used in various contexts to address conflicts, repair harm, and build stronger relationships.

1. Definition of Circle Processes

- Structured Dialogue: Circle processes involve a structured dialogue facilitated in a circle format, where all participants have an equal opportunity to speak and be heard.

- Restorative Goals: The primary goals are to address the harm caused by conflict, promote accountability, and facilitate healing and reconciliation.

2. Key Principles of Circle Processes

- Equality and Respect: All participants in the circle are considered equal, and respect is a fundamental principle guiding the dialogue.

- Inclusivity and Participation: Circle processes are inclusive, encouraging participation from all affected parties, including victims, offenders, and community members.

- Shared Responsibility: The circle emphasizes shared responsibility for addressing harm and finding solutions, promoting collective ownership of the resolution process.

The Process of Circle Processes

The circle process involves several stages, each designed to facilitate effective communication, mutual understanding, and collaborative resolution.

1. Preparation

- Identifying Participants: Facilitators identify and invite participants, ensuring that all relevant parties, including victims, offenders, and community members, are included.

- Setting Ground Rules: Facilitators establish ground rules for the circle, ensuring that participants understand the principles of respect, confidentiality, and equality.

- Individual Preparation: Facilitators may meet individually with participants to explain the process, address any concerns, and prepare them for the circle.

2. Opening the Circle

- Introductions and Purpose: The circle begins with introductions and a statement of the purpose and goals of the meeting. Facilitators explain the process and the role of each participant.

- Establishing Trust: Icebreaker activities or initial sharing rounds may be used to establish trust and build a sense of community among participants.

3. Facilitated Dialogue

- Talking Piece: A talking piece is often used to ensure that each participant has an equal opportunity to speak. Only the person holding the talking piece may speak, promoting active listening and respectful dialogue.

- Sharing Stories: Participants share their stories, focusing on the impact of the conflict or harm. This allows for a deeper understanding of the emotional, psychological, and social effects on all parties.

- Exploring Solutions: The circle facilitates a collaborative exploration of solutions, encouraging participants to propose and discuss ways to address the harm and promote healing.

4. Developing Agreements

- Consensus Building: Participants work together to develop agreements that outline specific actions to address the harm, promote healing, and prevent future conflicts.

- Commitment to Action: The agreements are based on consensus, with all participants committing to the actions outlined in the plan.

5. Closing the Circle

- Reflection and Gratitude: The circle concludes with a reflection on the process and expressions of gratitude from participants. Facilitators ensure that everyone feels heard and respected.

- Follow-Up Plans: Facilitators may outline follow-up plans to monitor the implementation of the agreements and provide ongoing support if needed.

Benefits of Circle Processes

Circle processes offer numerous benefits for victims, offenders, and the broader community. They promote healing, accountability, and social cohesion.

1. Benefits for Victims

- Empowerment and Voice: Circles provide victims with a platform to express their feelings, ask questions, and have a say in the resolution process.

- Emotional Healing: The supportive environment and acknowledgment of harm by the offender contribute to the victim's emotional healing and sense of justice.

- Restitution and Support: Victims receive tangible restitution and support from the offender and community, addressing their material and emotional needs.

2. Benefits for Offenders

- Accountability and Responsibility: Circles encourage offenders to take responsibility for their actions, understand the impact of their behavior, and make amends.

- Supportive Environment: The involvement of community members provides a supportive environment for the offender's rehabilitation and reintegration.

- Personal Growth: The process promotes personal growth, empathy, and positive behavioral change, reducing the likelihood of reoffending.

3. Benefits for the Community

- Strengthened Relationships: Circles foster stronger relationships within communities, promoting mutual support and collective responsibility.

- Social Harmony: The process helps restore social harmony by addressing the underlying harm and promoting reconciliation between victims, offenders, and the community.

- Alternative to Traditional Justice: Circles provide an alternative to the traditional justice system, offering a more restorative and community-based approach to addressing harm.

Case Studies and Examples

Examining real-life examples of circle processes highlights the effectiveness and impact of the practice in various contexts.

1. School-Based Circles

- Case Study: In a school setting, a circle was used to address a bullying incident involving several students. The circle included the victims, the offender, their peers, and school staff.

- Outcome: The offender expressed remorse, apologized, and agreed to participate in a peer mentoring program. The victims felt heard and supported, and the school community developed a plan to prevent future bullying.

2. Community Disputes

- Case Study: In a community affected by a series of neighborhood disputes, a circle was convened to bring together the involved parties and other community members.

- Outcome: Participants shared their experiences and concerns, leading to a deeper understanding of the issues. They developed a community agreement to promote better communication and conflict resolution practices.

3. Family Conflicts

- Case Study: In a case of a family conflict involving a teenage offender and their parents, a circle was used to facilitate dialogue and develop a plan for resolution.

- Outcome: The teenager took responsibility for their actions and agreed to participate in family counseling. The family developed a plan for improving communication and support, fostering a more positive home environment.

Challenges and Considerations in Circle Processes

While circle processes offer significant benefits, they also present several challenges and considerations that must be addressed to ensure their effectiveness and fairness.

1. Ensuring Voluntary Participation

- Genuine Consent: For circles to be effective, participation must be truly voluntary. Coercion or pressure to participate can undermine the sincerity and outcomes of the process.

- Informed Decision-Making: Participants must be fully informed about the process and its potential outcomes before agreeing to participate.

2. Addressing Power Imbalances

- Equitable Participation: Power imbalances between participants can affect the fairness and effectiveness of the circle. Facilitators must be skilled in addressing and mitigating these imbalances to ensure a balanced dialogue.

- Support and Advocacy: Providing support and advocacy for vulnerable participants can help address power imbalances and ensure that all voices are heard and respected.

3. Creating a Safe Environment

- Safety Concerns: Ensuring the physical and emotional safety of all participants is paramount. Facilitators must create a safe and respectful environment for the dialogue.

- Emotional Support: Providing access to emotional support and counseling for participants can help them process their feelings and engage more fully in the circle.

4. Cultural Sensitivity

- Respecting Diversity: Circles must be culturally sensitive and appropriate for the participants involved. Facilitators should be trained to understand and respect cultural differences and adapt the process accordingly.

- Community Engagement: Engaging with community leaders and members can help ensure that the circle process is respectful of and responsive to cultural norms and values.

Conclusion

Circle processes are a powerful restorative justice practice that promotes healing, accountability, and the restoration of relationships. By involving victims, offenders, and community members in a structured, inclusive dialogue, circles address the harm caused by conflicts, empower participants, support offender rehabilitation, and foster social cohesion. While promoting circle processes presents challenges, the collaborative and inclusive nature of the practice helps ensure that it is meaningful and effective. In the chapters that follow, we will continue to explore various restorative practices and models, delving into their principles, processes, and impacts in creating a more just and compassionate society.

Community Restorative Boards: Community-Driven Justice Practices

Community Restorative Boards (CRBs) are a key component of restorative justice, emphasizing the role of community members in addressing harm, supporting victims, and promoting offender accountability. This chapter explores the principles, processes, and benefits of Community Restorative Boards, as well as their broader impact on individuals and communities.

Understanding Community Restorative Boards

Community Restorative Boards involve local community members in the justice process, providing a forum for resolving conflicts, addressing harm, and supporting the rehabilitation of offenders. These boards are designed to foster a sense of collective responsibility and community engagement.

1. Definition of Community Restorative Boards

- Community-Driven Process: CRBs are composed of community volunteers who facilitate the resolution of conflicts and harms within their community.

- Restorative Goals: The primary goals are to address the harm caused by offenses, promote accountability, and facilitate healing and reintegration.

2. Key Principles of Community Restorative Boards

- Community Involvement: CRBs emphasize the active involvement of community members in the justice process, recognizing their role in maintaining social harmony.

- Collective Responsibility: The boards operate on the principle of collective responsibility, where the community works together to support victims and offenders.

- Restorative Justice: CRBs are grounded in restorative justice principles, focusing on repairing harm, restoring relationships, and promoting healing.

The Process of Community Restorative Boards

The CRB process involves several stages, each designed to facilitate effective communication, mutual understanding, and collaborative resolution.

1. Referral and Intake

- Case Referral: Cases can be referred to CRBs by the justice system, schools, social services, or community organizations. The suitability of the case for CRB intervention is assessed, considering the willingness of the parties to participate.

- Intake Assessment: Board members conduct an intake assessment to gather information about the case, understand the perspectives of the parties involved, and prepare for the board meeting.

2. Preparation

- Pre-Meeting Preparation: Board members meet to discuss the case, establish ground rules, and plan the meeting. They ensure that all participants understand the process and are prepared to engage constructively.

- Engaging Participants: The facilitator contacts the victim, offender, and relevant community members to explain the process, address any concerns, and invite them to the meeting.

3. The Board Meeting

- Opening: The meeting begins with introductions and an explanation of the purpose and goals of the session. The facilitator outlines the ground rules for respectful and constructive dialogue.

- Sharing Perspectives: Participants share their perspectives on the offense, its impact, and their feelings. This stage allows for open communication and mutual understanding.

- Exploring Solutions: The board facilitates a collaborative exploration of solutions, encouraging participants to propose and discuss ways to address the harm and promote healing.

- Developing Agreements: The board works with participants to develop a restorative agreement, outlining specific actions the offender will take to make amends and support their rehabilitation.

4. Follow-Up

- Monitoring Implementation: Board members monitor the implementation of the restorative agreement, providing support and addressing any challenges that arise.

- Additional Meetings: Follow-up meetings may be held to review progress, make adjustments to the plan if necessary, and ensure that the outcomes are being achieved.

Benefits of Community Restorative Boards

Community Restorative Boards offer numerous benefits for victims, offenders, and the broader community. They promote healing, accountability, and social cohesion.

1. Benefits for Victims

   - Empowerment and Voice: CRBs provide victims with an opportunity to express their feelings, ask questions, and have a say in the resolution process.

   - Emotional Healing: The supportive environment and acknowledgment of harm by the offender contribute to the victim's emotional healing and sense of justice.

   - Restitution and Support: Victims receive tangible restitution and support from the offender and community, addressing their material and emotional needs.

2. Benefits for Offenders

   - Accountability and Responsibility: CRBs encourage offenders to take responsibility for their actions, understand the impact of their behavior, and make amends.

   - Supportive Environment: The involvement of community members provides a supportive environment for the offender's rehabilitation and reintegration.

   - Personal Growth: The process promotes personal growth, empathy, and positive behavioral change, reducing the likelihood of reoffending.

3. Benefits for the Community

- Strengthened Relationships: CRBs foster stronger relationships within communities, promoting mutual support and collective responsibility.

- Social Harmony: The process helps restore social harmony by addressing the underlying harm and promoting reconciliation between victims, offenders, and the community.

- Alternative to Traditional Justice: CRBs provide an alternative to the traditional justice system, offering a more restorative and community-based approach to addressing harm.

Case Studies and Examples

Examining real-life examples of Community Restorative Boards highlights the effectiveness and impact of the process in various contexts.

1. Juvenile Offenses

- Case Study: In a case involving a juvenile offender who committed vandalism, a CRB was used to facilitate a dialogue between the offender, the victim, and community members.

- Outcome: The offender expressed remorse, agreed to repair the damage, and participated in community service. The victim felt heard and supported, and the community members developed a plan to support the offender's positive behavior.

2. Neighborhood Disputes

- Case Study: In a community affected by ongoing neighborhood disputes, a CRB brought together the involved parties and other community members to address the issues.

- Outcome: Participants shared their experiences and concerns, leading to a deeper understanding of the issues. They developed a community agreement to promote better communication and conflict resolution practices.

3. School Incidents

- Case Study: In a school setting, a CRB addressed a conflict involving several students and staff members. The board included students, teachers, and parents.

- Outcome: The offenders apologized and agreed to participate in peer mediation programs. The victims received support from the school community, and the board developed a plan to prevent future incidents and improve the school climate.

Challenges and Considerations in Community Restorative Boards

While CRBs offer significant benefits, they also present several challenges and considerations that must be addressed to ensure their effectiveness and fairness.

1. Ensuring Voluntary Participation

- Genuine Consent: For CRBs to be effective, participation must be truly voluntary. Coercion or pressure to participate can undermine the sincerity and outcomes of the process.

- Informed Decision-Making: Participants must be fully informed about the process and its potential outcomes before agreeing to participate.

2. Addressing Power Imbalances

- Equitable Participation: Power imbalances between participants can affect the fairness and effectiveness of the board. Facilitators must be skilled in addressing and mitigating these imbalances to ensure a balanced dialogue.

- Support and Advocacy: Providing support and advocacy for vulnerable participants can help address power imbalances and ensure that all voices are heard and respected.

3. Creating a Safe Environment

- Safety Concerns: Ensuring the physical and emotional safety of all participants is paramount. Facilitators must create a safe and respectful environment for the dialogue.

- Emotional Support: Providing access to emotional support and counseling for participants can help them process their feelings and engage more fully in the board.

4. Cultural Sensitivity

- Respecting Diversity: CRBs must be culturally sensitive and appropriate for the participants involved. Facilitators should be trained to understand and respect cultural differences and adapt the process accordingly.

- Community Engagement: Engaging with community leaders and members can help ensure that the board process is respectful of and responsive to cultural norms and values.

Conclusion

Community Restorative Boards are a powerful restorative justice practice that promotes healing, accountability, and the restoration of relationships. By involving community members in the justice process, CRBs address the harm caused by conflicts, empower participants, support offender rehabilitation, and foster social cohesion. While promoting CRBs presents challenges, the collaborative and inclusive nature of the practice helps ensure that it is meaningful and effective. In the chapters that follow, we will continue to explore various restorative practices and models, delving into their principles, processes, and impacts in creating a more just and compassionate society.

CHAPTER 05

CASE STUDIES AND REAL-WORLD APPLICATIONS

Criminal Justice System: Implementation of Restorative Practices in Criminal Justice

The implementation of restorative practices in the criminal justice system represents a significant shift from traditional punitive approaches to more holistic, community-centered methods of addressing crime. This chapter explores how restorative practices have been integrated into the criminal justice system, the benefits they offer, and the challenges they face. Through case studies and real-world examples, we will examine the impact of restorative justice on victims, offenders, and communities.

Understanding Restorative Practices in Criminal Justice

Restorative justice in the criminal justice system involves practices that prioritize healing, accountability, and the restoration of relationships over punishment. These practices aim to address the harm caused by crime and to rehabilitate offenders while involving the community in the justice process.

1. Key Principles of Restorative Practices

- Victim-Centered Approach: Restorative practices focus on addressing the needs and experiences of victims, providing them with a voice and an opportunity for healing.

- Offender Accountability: Offenders are encouraged to take responsibility for their actions, understand the impact of their behavior, and actively participate in making amends.

- Community Involvement: The community plays a vital role in supporting victims, holding offenders accountable, and fostering social cohesion and healing.

2. Types of Restorative Practices in Criminal Justice

- Victim-Offender Mediation (VOM): A facilitated dialogue between victims and offenders to address harm, promote understanding, and agree on reparative actions.

- Restorative Circles: Inclusive meetings involving victims, offenders, and community members to discuss the impact of the crime and develop a plan for resolution.

- Family Group Conferencing (FGC): Meetings that involve the victim, offender, their families, and community members to collaboratively address the harm and support rehabilitation.

- Community Restorative Boards (CRBs): Community-driven boards that facilitate restorative justice processes and monitor the implementation of agreements.

Benefits of Restorative Practices in Criminal Justice

The integration of restorative practices into the criminal justice system offers numerous benefits for victims, offenders, and communities.

1. Benefits for Victims

- Empowerment and Voice: Restorative practices provide victims with an opportunity to express their feelings, ask questions, and participate in the justice process.

- Emotional Healing: Victims receive emotional support and validation, facilitating their healing and recovery from the trauma of the crime.

- Restitution and Reparation: Victims can negotiate restitution and reparation, addressing their material and emotional needs.

2. Benefits for Offenders

- Accountability and Responsibility: Restorative practices encourage offenders to take responsibility for their actions and understand the impact of their behavior on others.

- Personal Growth and Rehabilitation: The process promotes personal growth, empathy, and positive behavioral change, reducing the likelihood of reoffending.

- Supportive Reintegration: Offenders receive support from their community, aiding their rehabilitation and reintegration into society.

3. Benefits for the Community

- Strengthened Social Bonds: Restorative practices foster stronger relationships within communities, promoting mutual support and collective responsibility.

- Social Harmony and Cohesion: The process helps restore social harmony by addressing the underlying harm and promoting reconciliation between victims, offenders, and the community.

- Alternative to Traditional Justice: Restorative practices provide an alternative to the traditional justice system, offering a more humane and community-based approach to addressing crime.

Case Studies and Examples

Examining real-life examples of restorative practices in the criminal justice system highlights their effectiveness and impact.

1. New Zealand's Restorative Justice Programs

- Background: New Zealand has been a pioneer in integrating restorative justice into its criminal justice system, particularly through Family Group Conferencing (FGC).

- Implementation: FGCs are used extensively in cases involving juvenile offenders. The process brings together the victim, offender, their families, and community representatives to discuss the harm caused and develop a plan for making amends.

- Outcome: Studies have shown that FGCs in New Zealand lead to higher levels of victim satisfaction, reduced recidivism rates, and improved rehabilitation outcomes for offenders.

2. Canada's Victim-Offender Mediation Programs

- Background: Canada has implemented victim-offender mediation (VOM) programs in various jurisdictions, focusing on both juvenile and adult offenders.

- Implementation: VOM sessions are facilitated by trained mediators and involve direct dialogue between victims and offenders to address the harm and agree on reparative actions.

- Outcome: Research indicates that VOM programs in Canada result in high levels of victim satisfaction, increased offender accountability, and lower recidivism rates compared to traditional justice processes.

3. United States Community Restorative Boards

- Background: Community Restorative Boards (CRBs) have been established in several states across the United States to address minor offenses and support offender rehabilitation.

- Implementation: CRBs involve community volunteers who facilitate restorative processes, develop reparative agreements, and monitor their implementation.

- Outcome: CRBs have been effective in promoting community involvement, reducing reoffending rates, and fostering social cohesion and support for both victims and offenders.

4. South Africa's Truth and Reconciliation Commission (TRC)

- Background: South Africa's Truth and Reconciliation Commission (TRC) was established to address the atrocities committed during apartheid and promote national healing.

- Implementation: The TRC facilitated public hearings where victims and perpetrators could share their experiences, seek forgiveness, and agree on reparative actions.

- Outcome: The TRC played a crucial role in promoting reconciliation and healing in South Africa, providing a model for restorative justice processes in post-conflict societies.

Challenges and Considerations in Implementing Restorative Practices

While restorative practices offer significant benefits, their implementation in the criminal justice system presents several challenges and considerations.

1. Ensuring Voluntary Participation

- Genuine Consent: Participation in restorative practices must be truly voluntary. Coercion or pressure to participate can undermine the sincerity and outcomes of the process.

- Informed Decision-Making: Participants must be fully informed about the process and its potential outcomes before agreeing to participate.

2. Addressing Power Imbalances

- Equitable Participation: Power imbalances between victims and offenders can affect the fairness and effectiveness of restorative processes. Facilitators must be skilled in addressing and mitigating these imbalances to ensure a balanced dialogue.

- Support and Advocacy: Providing support and advocacy for vulnerable participants can help address power imbalances and ensure that all voices are heard and respected.

3. Creating a Safe Environment

- Safety Concerns: Ensuring the physical and emotional safety of all participants is paramount. Facilitators must create a safe and respectful environment for the dialogue.

- Emotional Support: Providing access to emotional support and counseling for participants can help them process their feelings and engage more fully in the process.

4. Cultural Sensitivity

- Respecting Diversity: Restorative practices must be culturally sensitive and appropriate for the participants involved. Facilitators should be trained to understand and respect cultural differences and adapt the process accordingly.

- Community Engagement: Engaging with community leaders and members can help ensure that restorative processes are respectful of and responsive to cultural norms and values.

5. Sustainability and Integration

- Institutional Support: Successful implementation of restorative practices requires institutional support, including training for facilitators, funding for programs, and policies that integrate restorative approaches into the criminal justice system.

- Ongoing Evaluation: Regular evaluation and assessment of restorative practices are essential to ensure their effectiveness, address challenges, and improve processes.

Conclusion

The integration of restorative practices into the criminal justice system represents a transformative shift towards a more holistic, community-centered approach to justice. By focusing on healing, accountability, and the restoration of relationships, restorative practices offer significant benefits for victims, offenders, and communities. While implementing these practices presents challenges, the collaborative and inclusive nature of restorative justice helps ensure that the process is meaningful and effective. In the chapters that follow, we will continue to explore various restorative practices and models, delving into their principles, processes, and impacts in creating a more just and compassionate society.

Schools and Educational Settings: Restorative Justice in Schools and Its Impact on Students

Restorative justice in schools and educational settings focuses on creating a supportive and inclusive environment where conflicts are resolved through dialogue, accountability, and mutual respect. This chapter explores the implementation of restorative practices in schools, their benefits, and the challenges they face. Through case studies and real-world examples, we will examine the impact of restorative justice on students, teachers, and school communities.

Understanding Restorative Justice in Schools

Restorative justice in schools involves practices that prioritize repairing harm, fostering understanding, and promoting a positive school climate. These practices aim to address disciplinary issues, improve student behavior, and build a supportive school community.

1. Key Principles of Restorative Justice in Schools

- Respect and Dignity: Restorative practices emphasize treating all students with respect and dignity, recognizing their inherent worth.

- Accountability and Responsibility: Students are encouraged to take responsibility for their actions, understand the impact of their behavior, and make amends.

- Community and Relationships: Building strong, positive relationships within the school community is a central focus, fostering a sense of belonging and mutual support.

2. Types of Restorative Practices in Schools

- Restorative Circles: Regularly scheduled circles where students and teachers discuss issues, resolve conflicts, and build community.

- Peer Mediation: Trained student mediators help their peers resolve conflicts through guided dialogue and problem-solving.

- Restorative Conferences: Facilitated meetings involving students, teachers, and sometimes parents to address specific incidents of harm and develop plans for resolution.

- Restorative Dialogue: One-on-one or small group discussions to address conflicts and misunderstandings, promoting empathy and understanding.

Benefits of Restorative Justice in Schools

Implementing restorative practices in schools offers numerous benefits for students, teachers, and the broader school community.

1. Benefits for Students

- Improved Behavior: Restorative practices encourage students to reflect on their actions, understand their impact, and develop better behavior.

- Enhanced Social Skills: Students learn important social and emotional skills, such as empathy, active listening, and conflict resolution.

- Increased Engagement: A positive and supportive school environment increases student engagement, leading to better academic performance and school attendance.

- Reduced Bullying: Restorative practices address the underlying causes of bullying and promote a culture of respect and inclusion.

2. Benefits for Teachers

- Better Classroom Management: Restorative practices provide teachers with tools to manage classroom behavior effectively, reducing disruptions and creating a more positive learning environment.

- Stronger Relationships: Teachers build stronger, more trusting relationships with students, fostering a collaborative and supportive classroom culture.

- Professional Development: Implementing restorative practices involves ongoing training and professional development for teachers, enhancing their skills and confidence in handling conflicts.

3. Benefits for the School Community

- Positive School Climate: Restorative practices contribute to a positive school climate, where students feel safe, respected, and valued.

- Community Involvement: Engaging parents and community members in restorative processes strengthens the school community and fosters a sense of collective responsibility.

- Alternative to Punitive Discipline: Restorative practices offer an alternative to punitive disciplinary measures, such as suspensions and expulsions, promoting more equitable and effective responses to student behavior.

Case Studies and Examples

Examining real-life examples of restorative practices in schools highlights their effectiveness and impact on the school community.

1. Restorative Circles at Edward W. Brooke Charter School

- Background: Edward W. Brooke Charter School in Boston, Massachusetts, implemented restorative circles to address behavioral issues and build a positive school culture.

- Implementation: The school scheduled regular restorative circles, where students and teachers discussed issues, shared feelings, and resolved conflicts collaboratively.

- Outcome: The implementation of restorative circles led to a significant decrease in disciplinary referrals and suspensions, improved student behavior, and a more supportive and inclusive school environment.

2. Peer Mediation Program at West Philadelphia High School

- Background: West Philadelphia High School introduced a peer mediation program to address conflicts and reduce violence among students.

- Implementation: Trained student mediators facilitated mediation sessions, helping their peers resolve conflicts through guided dialogue and problem-solving.

- Outcome: The peer mediation program resulted in a reduction in fights and violent incidents, improved relationships among students, and increased student leadership and responsibility.

3. Restorative Conferences at Denver Public Schools

- Background: Denver Public Schools implemented restorative conferences as part of their discipline policy to address serious behavioral incidents.

- Implementation: Restorative conferences involved students, teachers, and sometimes parents in facilitated meetings to discuss the incident, its impact, and develop a plan for making amends.

- Outcome: The use of restorative conferences led to a decrease in suspensions and expulsions, improved student behavior, and a greater sense of accountability and responsibility among students.

4. Whole-School Restorative Approach at Oakland Unified School District

- Background: Oakland Unified School District adopted a whole-school restorative approach to create a positive and supportive school climate.

- Implementation: The district provided extensive training for staff, integrated restorative practices into the curriculum, and engaged parents and community members in the process.

- Outcome: The whole-school restorative approach resulted in a significant decrease in disciplinary actions, improved academic outcomes, and a more inclusive and supportive school environment.

Challenges and Considerations in Implementing Restorative Practices

While restorative practices offer significant benefits, their implementation in schools presents several challenges and considerations.

1. Ensuring Buy-In and Support

- Staff and Student Buy-In: Successful implementation requires buy-in and support from both staff and students. Building understanding and commitment to restorative principles is essential.

- Leadership Support: Strong support from school leadership is crucial for providing the necessary resources, training, and policy changes to implement restorative practices effectively.

2. Providing Training and Professional Development

- Ongoing Training: Implementing restorative practices requires ongoing training and professional development for teachers, staff, and students to build the necessary skills and confidence.

- Resource Allocation: Schools must allocate resources for training, facilitation, and support to ensure the sustainability of restorative practices.

3. Addressing Power Imbalances

- Equitable Participation: Power imbalances between students, teachers, and other participants can affect the fairness and effectiveness of restorative processes. Facilitators must be skilled in addressing and mitigating these imbalances.

- Support and Advocacy: Providing support and advocacy for vulnerable students can help address power imbalances and ensure that all voices are heard and respected.

4. Creating a Safe Environment

- Physical and Emotional Safety: Ensuring the physical and emotional safety of all participants is paramount. Facilitators must create a safe and respectful environment for restorative dialogue.

- Emotional Support: Providing access to emotional support and counseling for students can help them process their feelings and engage more fully in restorative practices.

5. Cultural Sensitivity

- Respecting Diversity: Restorative practices must be culturally sensitive and appropriate for the diverse student population. Facilitators should be trained to understand and respect cultural differences and adapt the process accordingly.

- Community Engagement: Engaging parents and community members can help ensure that restorative practices are respectful of and responsive to cultural norms and values.

Conclusion

Restorative justice in schools and educational settings offers a transformative approach to addressing conflicts, improving student behavior, and building a supportive school community. By focusing on healing, accountability, and relationships, restorative practices create a positive school climate where students feel safe, respected, and valued. While implementing these practices presents challenges, the collaborative and inclusive nature of restorative justice helps ensure that the process is meaningful and effective. In the chapters that follow, we will continue to explore various restorative practices and models, delving into their principles, processes, and impacts in creating a more just and compassionate society.

Workplace and Organizations: Restorative Approaches in Resolving Workplace Conflicts

Restorative justice practices are increasingly being implemented in workplaces and organizations to address conflicts, foster a positive work environment, and improve employee relations. This chapter explores the principles, processes, and benefits of restorative approaches in resolving workplace conflicts, alongside case studies and real-world examples demonstrating their impact.

Understanding Restorative Approaches in the Workplace

Restorative approaches in the workplace focus on repairing harm, promoting understanding, and restoring relationships. These methods are used to address various conflicts, ranging from interpersonal disputes to systemic issues within the organization.

1. Key Principles of Restorative Approaches

- Respect and Dignity: Treating all employees with respect and recognizing their inherent worth.

- Accountability and Responsibility: Encouraging employees to take responsibility for their actions and their impact on others.

- Community and Relationships: Building strong, positive relationships within the workplace community to foster a sense of belonging and mutual support.

2. Types of Restorative Practices in the Workplace

- Restorative Circles: Facilitated meetings where employees can discuss issues, resolve conflicts, and build community.

- Mediation: A neutral third party helps conflicting parties reach a mutually acceptable resolution through guided dialogue.

- Restorative Conferences: Structured meetings involving the parties in conflict, their supporters, and a facilitator to address harm and develop a plan for making amends.

- Restorative Dialogue: One-on-one or small group discussions to address conflicts and misunderstandings, promoting empathy and understanding.

Benefits of Restorative Approaches in the Workplace

Implementing restorative practices in the workplace offers numerous benefits for employees, managers, and the organization as a whole.

1. Benefits for Employees

- Improved Relationships: Restorative practices help repair and strengthen relationships among employees, fostering a more collaborative and supportive work environment.

- Enhanced Communication Skills: Employees develop better communication and conflict resolution skills, leading to more effective teamwork and collaboration.

- Increased Engagement and Morale: A positive and inclusive workplace culture increases employee engagement and morale, reducing turnover and absenteeism.

- Addressing Workplace Harassment: Restorative practices provide a platform for addressing and resolving issues related to workplace harassment and discrimination in a constructive manner.

2. Benefits for Managers

- Effective Conflict Resolution: Restorative approaches equip managers with tools to handle conflicts effectively, reducing the time and resources spent on unresolved disputes.

- Positive Leadership: Managers who use restorative practices build trust and credibility with their teams, fostering a more positive and productive work environment.

- Professional Development: Implementing restorative practices involves ongoing training and professional development for managers, enhancing their leadership skills and confidence.

3. Benefits for the Organization

- Improved Organizational Culture: Restorative practices contribute to a positive organizational culture, where employees feel valued, respected, and heard.

- Enhanced Productivity: A supportive and harmonious work environment leads to increased productivity and overall organizational performance.

- Reduced Legal Risks: Addressing conflicts through restorative practices can help prevent escalation to legal disputes, reducing the risk of costly litigation.

- Corporate Social Responsibility: Organizations that implement restorative practices demonstrate a commitment to ethical and socially responsible business practices.

Case Studies and Examples

Examining real-life examples of restorative practices in the workplace highlights their effectiveness and impact on the organization.

1. Restorative Circles at Google

- Background: Google implemented restorative circles to address interpersonal conflicts and improve team dynamics within its diverse workforce.

- Implementation: Facilitated by trained mediators, restorative circles provided a safe space for employees to discuss issues, share feelings, and collaboratively find solutions.

- Outcome: The use of restorative circles led to improved communication, stronger team relationships, and increased employee satisfaction and engagement.

2. Mediation Program at Coca-Cola

- Background: Coca-Cola introduced a mediation program to resolve workplace conflicts and promote a positive organizational culture.

- Implementation: Trained mediators facilitated confidential mediation sessions, helping employees address conflicts and develop mutually acceptable resolutions.

- Outcome: The mediation program resulted in a significant reduction in formal grievances and disciplinary actions, as well as improved employee relations and job satisfaction.

3. Restorative Conferences at Kaiser Permanente

- Background: Kaiser Permanente implemented restorative conferences to address incidents of workplace harassment and discrimination.

- Implementation: Restorative conferences involved the parties in conflict, their supporters, and a facilitator in structured meetings to discuss the impact of the harm and develop a plan for making amends.

- Outcome: The use of restorative conferences led to a decrease in harassment complaints, improved workplace climate, and enhanced trust between employees and management.

4. Whole-Organization Restorative Approach at Patagonia

- Background: Patagonia adopted a whole-organization restorative approach to create a supportive and inclusive workplace culture.

- Implementation: The company provided extensive training for staff, integrated restorative practices into its policies and procedures, and engaged employees in regular restorative circles and dialogues.

- Outcome: The whole-organization restorative approach resulted in increased employee engagement, higher retention rates, and a stronger, more cohesive organizational culture.

Challenges and Considerations in Implementing Restorative Practices

While restorative practices offer significant benefits, their implementation in the workplace presents several challenges and considerations.

1. Ensuring Buy-In and Support

- Employee and Management Buy-In: Successful implementation requires buy-in and support from both employees and management. Building understanding and commitment to restorative principles is essential.

- Leadership Support: Strong support from organizational leadership is crucial for providing the necessary resources, training, and policy changes to implement restorative practices effectively.

2. Providing Training and Professional Development

- Ongoing Training: Implementing restorative practices requires ongoing training and professional development for employees and managers to build the necessary skills and confidence.

- Resource Allocation: Organizations must allocate resources for training, facilitation, and support to ensure the sustainability of restorative practices.

3. Addressing Power Imbalances

- Equitable Participation: Power imbalances between employees, managers, and other participants can affect the fairness and effectiveness of restorative processes. Facilitators must be skilled in addressing and mitigating these imbalances.

- Support and Advocacy: Providing support and advocacy for vulnerable employees can help address power imbalances and ensure that all voices are heard and respected.

4. Creating a Safe Environment

- Physical and Emotional Safety: Ensuring the physical and emotional safety of all participants is paramount. Facilitators must create a safe and respectful environment for restorative dialogue.

- Emotional Support: Providing access to emotional support and counseling for employees can help them process their feelings and engage more fully in restorative practices.

5. Cultural Sensitivity

- Respecting Diversity: Restorative practices must be culturally sensitive and appropriate for the diverse employee population. Facilitators should be trained to understand and respect cultural differences and adapt the process accordingly.

- Community Engagement: Engaging with community leaders and members can help ensure that restorative practices are respectful of and responsive to cultural norms and values.

Conclusion

Restorative justice practices in the workplace offer a transformative approach to addressing conflicts, improving employee relations, and building a supportive organizational culture. By focusing on healing, accountability, and relationships, restorative practices create a positive work environment where employees feel valued, respected, and heard. While implementing these practices presents challenges, the collaborative and inclusive nature of restorative justice helps ensure that the process is meaningful and effective. In the chapters that follow, we will continue to explore various restorative practices and models, delving into their principles, processes, and impacts in creating a more just and compassionate society.

Community Programs: Successful Community-Based Restorative Justice Programs

Community-based restorative justice programs play a crucial role in addressing harm, fostering healing, and promoting social cohesion. These programs are designed to engage community members in resolving conflicts, supporting victims, and rehabilitating offenders. This chapter explores the principles, processes, and benefits of successful community-based restorative justice programs through case studies and real-world examples.

Understanding Community-Based Restorative Justice Programs

Community-based restorative justice programs emphasize the active involvement of community members in the justice process. These programs are rooted in the belief that the community plays a vital role in maintaining social harmony and addressing harm.

1. Key Principles of Community-Based Restorative Justice

- Community Involvement: The active participation of community members is essential in addressing harm and supporting the justice process.

- Restorative Justice: Focuses on repairing harm, promoting accountability, and facilitating healing for all parties involved.

- Collective Responsibility: Encourages a sense of collective responsibility, where the community works together to support victims and offenders.

2. Types of Community-Based Restorative Justice Programs

- Restorative Circles: Facilitated meetings where community members, victims, and offenders discuss issues, resolve conflicts, and build community.

- Community Restorative Boards: Boards composed of community volunteers who facilitate restorative processes and monitor the implementation of agreements.

- Family Group Conferencing: Meetings involving the victim, offender, their families, and community members to collaboratively address harm and support rehabilitation.

Victim-Offender Mediation: Facilitated dialogues between victims and offenders to address harm, promote understanding, and agree on reparative actions.

Benefits of Community-Based Restorative Justice Programs

Implementing restorative justice programs at the community level offers numerous benefits for victims, offenders, and the broader community.

1. Benefits for Victims

- Empowerment and Voice: Victims have the opportunity to express their feelings, ask questions, and participate actively in the justice process.

- Emotional Healing: The supportive environment and acknowledgment of harm by the offender contribute to the victim's emotional healing and sense of justice.

- Restitution and Support: Victims receive tangible restitution and support from the offender and community, addressing their material and emotional needs.

2. Benefits for Offenders

- Accountability and Responsibility: Offenders are encouraged to take responsibility for their actions, understand the impact of their behavior and make amends.

- Supportive Environment: The involvement of community members provides a supportive environment for the offender's rehabilitation and reintegration.

- Personal Growth: The process promotes personal growth, empathy, and positive behavioral change, reducing the likelihood of reoffending.

3. Benefits for the Community

- Strengthened Social Bonds: Community-based programs foster stronger relationships within communities, promoting mutual support and collective responsibility.

- Social Harmony: The process helps restore social harmony by addressing the underlying harm and promoting reconciliation between victims, offenders, and the community.

- Alternative to Traditional Justice: These programs provide an alternative to the traditional justice system, offering a more restorative and community-based approach to addressing harm.

Case Studies and Examples

Examining real-life examples of successful community-based restorative justice programs highlights their effectiveness and impact on the community.

1. Community Restorative Boards in Vermont

- Background: Vermont has implemented Community Restorative Boards (CRBs) as part of its restorative justice initiatives, involving community volunteers in addressing low-level offenses.

- Implementation: CRBs facilitate restorative processes, develop reparative agreements, and monitor their implementation. They involve victims, offenders, and community members in the dialogue and resolution process.

- Outcome: CRBs in Vermont have led to reduced recidivism rates, increased victim satisfaction, and stronger community engagement and support.

2. Restorative Circles in Brazil

- Background: Brazil has adopted restorative circles in various communities to address conflicts and promote social harmony.

- Implementation: Facilitated by trained mediators, restorative circles bring together community members, victims, and offenders to discuss issues, share feelings, and collaboratively find solutions.

- Outcome: The use of restorative circles has resulted in improved communication, stronger community relationships, and effective conflict resolution, contributing to a decrease in violence and crime.

3. Family Group Conferencing in New Zealand

- Background: New Zealand is a pioneer in implementing Family Group Conferencing (FGC) as a central component of its juvenile justice system.

- Implementation: FGC involves the victim, offender, their families, and community members in meetings to discuss the harm, its impact, and develop a plan for making amends and supporting the offender's rehabilitation.

- Outcome: FGC in New Zealand has led to higher levels of victim satisfaction, reduced recidivism rates, and better rehabilitation outcomes for young offenders.

4. Victim-Offender Mediation in Canada

- Background: Canada has implemented victim-offender mediation (VOM) programs across various jurisdictions, focusing on both juvenile and adult offenders.

- Implementation: VOM sessions are facilitated by trained mediators and involve direct dialogue between victims and offenders to address harm and agree on reparative actions.

- Outcome: VOM programs in Canada have shown high levels of victim satisfaction, increased offender accountability, and lower recidivism rates compared to traditional justice processes.

Challenges and Considerations in Implementing Community-Based Programs

While community-based restorative justice programs offer significant benefits, their implementation presents several challenges and considerations.

1. Ensuring Voluntary Participation

- Genuine Consent: Participation in restorative processes must be truly voluntary. Coercion or pressure to participate can undermine the sincerity and outcomes of the process.

- Informed Decision-Making: Participants must be fully informed about the process and its potential outcomes before agreeing to participate.

2. Addressing Power Imbalances

- Equitable Participation: Power imbalances between participants can affect the fairness and effectiveness of restorative processes. Facilitators must be skilled in addressing and mitigating these imbalances.

- Support and Advocacy: Providing support and advocacy for vulnerable participants can help address power imbalances and ensure that all voices are heard and respected.

3. Creating a Safe Environment

- Safety Concerns: Ensuring the physical and emotional safety of all participants is paramount. Facilitators must create a safe and respectful environment for the dialogue.

- Emotional Support: Providing access to emotional support and counseling for participants can help them process their feelings and engage more fully in restorative practices.

4. Cultural Sensitivity

- Respecting Diversity: Restorative practices must be culturally sensitive and appropriate for the diverse community population. Facilitators should be trained to understand and respect cultural differences and adapt the process accordingly.

- Community Engagement: Engaging with community leaders and members can help ensure that restorative practices are respectful of and responsive to cultural norms and values.

5. Sustainability and Integration

- Institutional Support: Successful implementation of community-based programs requires institutional support, including training for facilitators, funding for programs, and policies that integrate restorative approaches into the community justice system.

- Ongoing Evaluation: Regular evaluation and assessment of restorative programs are essential to ensure their effectiveness, address challenges, and improve processes.

Conclusion

Community-based restorative justice programs offer a transformative approach to addressing harm, fostering healing, and promoting social cohesion. By actively involving community members in the justice process, these programs create a supportive environment where victims feel empowered, offenders are held accountable, and communities are strengthened. While implementing these programs presents challenges, the collaborative and inclusive nature of restorative justice helps ensure that the process is meaningful and effective. In the chapters that follow, we will continue to explore various restorative practices and models, delving into their principles, processes, and impacts in creating a more just and compassionate society.

CHAPTER 06

BENEFITS AND CHALLENGES

Positive Outcomes: Evidence of the Benefits of Restorative Justice for Victims, Offenders, and Communities

Restorative justice has demonstrated significant benefits for victims, offenders, and communities, offering a more holistic and effective approach to addressing harm and promoting healing. This chapter delves into the positive outcomes of restorative justice, supported by evidence and real-world examples, highlighting how these practices contribute to the well-being and harmony of all parties involved.

Positive Outcomes for Victims

Restorative justice practices prioritize the needs and experiences of victims, providing them with a platform for healing, empowerment, and closure.

1. Empowerment and Voice

- Active Participation: Restorative justice processes actively involve victims, giving them a voice in the justice process. Victims have the opportunity to express their feelings, ask questions, and influence the resolution.

- Validation of Experience: Victims feel heard and validated when their experiences and emotions are acknowledged by the offender and the community.

2. Emotional Healing

- Closure: Participating in restorative justice processes helps victims achieve closure by understanding the reasons behind the offender's actions and receiving apologies and reparative actions.

- Reduction of Trauma: The supportive and empathetic environment of restorative justice can help reduce the trauma associated with the crime, promoting emotional healing and recovery.

3. Restitution and Support

- Material Restitution: Victims can negotiate material restitution, such as financial compensation or the return of stolen property, addressing their immediate needs and losses.

- Community Support: The involvement of community members in the restorative process provides victims with a network of support, helping them rebuild their lives and regain a sense of security.

Positive Outcomes for Offenders

Restorative justice emphasizes accountability and rehabilitation for offenders, encouraging them to take responsibility for their actions and make positive changes.

1. Accountability and Responsibility

- Acknowledgment of Harm: Offenders are encouraged to acknowledge the harm they have caused and understand its impact on the victim and the community.

- Taking Responsibility: The process promotes a sense of responsibility, where offenders actively participate in making amends and repairing the harm.

2. Personal Growth and Rehabilitation

- Empathy and Remorse: Restorative justice fosters empathy and remorse, helping offenders develop a deeper understanding of the consequences of their actions.

- Behavioral Change: The focus on rehabilitation and personal growth encourages offenders to change their behavior, reducing the likelihood of reoffending and supporting their reintegration into society.

3. Supportive Reintegration

- Community Support: Offenders receive support from the community and restorative justice facilitators, aiding their reintegration and reducing the social stigma associated with their actions.

- Skills Development: Restorative processes often include elements of skills development and counseling, helping offenders build a positive future.

Positive Outcomes for Communities

Communities benefit from restorative justice through improved social cohesion, reduced crime rates, and a stronger sense of collective responsibility and support.

1. Strengthened Social Bonds

- Community Engagement: Restorative justice involves community members in the justice process, fostering a sense of collective responsibility and mutual support.

- Rebuilding Trust: The collaborative and inclusive nature of restorative practices helps rebuild trust within the community, promoting social harmony.

2. Reduced Crime Rates

- Preventing Recidivism: The focus on rehabilitation and accountability for offenders reduces recidivism rates, contributing to safer communities.

- Early Conflict Resolution: Restorative justice practices can address conflicts and minor offenses early, preventing escalation and reducing the overall crime rate.

3. Improved Community Well-Being

- Positive Community Culture: Restorative justice promotes a culture of respect, empathy, and support within the community, enhancing overall well-being.

- Empowerment of Community Members: Involving community members in the justice process empowers them to take an active role in maintaining social order and addressing harm.

Evidence of Positive Outcomes

The positive outcomes of restorative justice are supported by extensive research and real-world examples, demonstrating its effectiveness in various contexts.

1. Research Findings

- Victim Satisfaction: Studies consistently show high levels of victim satisfaction with restorative justice processes. Victims report feeling heard, respected, and more satisfied with the justice outcomes compared to traditional justice methods.

- Reduced Recidivism: Research indicates that restorative justice reduces recidivism rates among offenders. Programs such as Family Group Conferencing in New Zealand and Victim-Offender Mediation in Canada have demonstrated significant reductions in reoffending rates.

- Improved Community Relations: Evidence from restorative justice programs worldwide shows improved community relations, with increased trust and cooperation between community members and justice systems.

2. Real-World Examples

- New Zealand's Family Group Conferencing: This program has shown high levels of victim satisfaction, reduced recidivism rates, and better rehabilitation outcomes for young offenders.

- Canada's Victim-Offender Mediation: Canadian VOM programs have resulted in high victim satisfaction, increased offender accountability, and lower recidivism rates compared to traditional justice processes.

- South Africa's Truth and Reconciliation Commission: The TRC facilitated national healing and reconciliation, providing a model for restorative justice in post-conflict societies.

Challenges in Measuring Positive Outcomes

While restorative justice demonstrates numerous benefits, measuring these outcomes presents several challenges.

1. Subjective Experiences

- Variability in Perceptions: Victims and offenders may have different perceptions of satisfaction and healing, making it difficult to quantify outcomes consistently.

- Cultural Differences: Cultural differences can affect how restorative justice processes are perceived and experienced, influencing the reported outcomes.

2. Long-Term Impact

- Sustained Change: Measuring the long-term impact of restorative justice on behavior and community well-being requires ongoing evaluation and follow-up.

- Systemic Changes: Assessing the broader impact of restorative justice on the criminal justice system and societal norms involves complex, multi-faceted analysis.

3. Resource Allocation

- Funding and Support: Ensuring adequate funding and support for restorative justice programs is essential for their sustainability and effectiveness.

- Training and Professional Development: Ongoing training and professional development for facilitators and community members are crucial for maintaining the quality and integrity of restorative practices.

Conclusion

The positive outcomes of restorative justice for victims, offenders, and communities highlight its transformative potential as an alternative to traditional justice systems. By prioritizing healing, accountability, and community involvement, restorative justice fosters a more compassionate and effective approach to addressing harm and promoting social cohesion. While measuring these outcomes presents challenges, the evidence and real-world examples underscore the significant benefits of restorative justice practices. In the chapters that follow, we will continue to explore the challenges and limitations of restorative justice, as well as strategies for overcoming these obstacles to create a more just and compassionate society.

Common Challenges: Obstacles to Implementing Restorative Justice and Strategies to Overcome Them

While restorative justice offers numerous benefits, its implementation is not without challenges. This chapter explores the common obstacles to implementing restorative justice and presents strategies to overcome them. Understanding and addressing these challenges is crucial for the effective integration and sustainability of restorative practices.

Common Challenges in Implementing Restorative Justice

1. Resistance to Change

- Cultural and Institutional Resistance: Many justice systems and institutions are deeply rooted in retributive approaches. Shifting to a restorative model requires significant cultural and institutional change, which can encounter resistance from stakeholders accustomed to traditional methods.

- Lack of Awareness: There is often a lack of awareness and understanding of restorative justice among the public, policymakers, and practitioners, leading to skepticism and resistance.

2. Resource Constraints

- Funding Limitations: Implementing restorative justice programs requires funding for training, facilitation, and ongoing support. Limited financial resources can hinder the establishment and sustainability of these programs.

- Staffing and Training: Adequately trained facilitators are essential for the success of restorative practices. However, there is often a shortage of trained personnel, and providing comprehensive training can be resource-intensive.

3. Ensuring Voluntary Participation

- Genuine Consent: For restorative justice to be effective, participation must be voluntary. Coercion or pressure to participate can undermine the sincerity and outcomes of the process.

- Informed Decision-Making: Participants need to be fully informed about the process and its potential outcomes to make a genuine choice to engage.

4. Addressing Power Imbalances

- Equitable Participation: Power imbalances between victims and offenders, or within the community, can affect the fairness and effectiveness of restorative processes. These imbalances can stem from differences in social status, authority, or vulnerability.

- Support and Advocacy: Vulnerable participants, such as victims of severe trauma or marginalized individuals, may require additional support and advocacy to ensure their voices are heard and respected.

5. Creating a Safe Environment

- Physical and Emotional Safety: Ensuring the physical and emotional safety of all participants is paramount. Participants must feel secure and respected to engage fully in the process.

- Handling Emotional Intensity: Restorative justice processes can evoke strong emotions. Facilitators must be prepared to manage emotional intensity and provide support as needed.

6. Cultural Sensitivity

- Respecting Diversity: Restorative practices must be culturally sensitive and appropriate for the diverse populations they serve. Failure to consider cultural differences can lead to misunderstandings and ineffective outcomes.

- Community Engagement: Engaging community leaders and members in the design and implementation of restorative practices helps ensure cultural relevance and acceptance.

7. Sustainability and Integration

- Institutional Support: Successful implementation requires strong institutional support, including policies that integrate restorative approaches into existing justice systems.

- Ongoing Evaluation: Regular evaluation and assessment of restorative programs are essential to ensure their effectiveness, address challenges, and improve processes.

Strategies to Overcome Challenges

1. Building Awareness and Support

- Education and Training: Conducting educational campaigns and providing training for justice professionals, community leaders, and the public can increase awareness and understanding of restorative justice.

- Advocacy and Policy Change: Advocating for policy changes that support restorative justice can help institutionalize these practices and secure necessary resources.

2. Securing Funding and Resources

- Funding Opportunities: Exploring diverse funding opportunities, including government grants, private donations, and community fundraising, can provide the financial resources needed to support restorative justice programs.

- Collaborative Partnerships: Building partnerships with community organizations, educational institutions, and businesses can enhance resource availability and support for restorative practices.

3. Ensuring Voluntary Participation

- Informed Consent: Providing clear, accessible information about the restorative process and its potential benefits and risks helps ensure that participation is genuinely voluntary.

- Creating Safe Spaces: Ensuring that the environment is safe and supportive can encourage voluntary participation and engagement.

4. Addressing Power Imbalances

- Skilled Facilitation: Training facilitators to recognize and address power imbalances is crucial. Facilitators should be skilled in creating an equitable environment where all participants feel heard and respected.

- Providing Support and Advocacy: Offering support services, such as counseling and advocacy, can help vulnerable participants engage more fully and confidently in the process.

5. Creating a Safe Environment

- Trauma-Informed Practices: Integrating trauma-informed practices into restorative processes can help ensure the physical and emotional safety of participants.

- Emotional Support Services: Providing access to emotional support and counseling during and after restorative sessions can help participants manage intense emotions.

6. Ensuring Cultural Sensitivity

- Cultural Competence Training: Training facilitators and practitioners in cultural competence ensures that restorative practices are respectful and appropriate for diverse populations.

- Community Involvement: Involving community leaders and members in the development and implementation of restorative programs can enhance cultural relevance and acceptance.

7. Promoting Sustainability and Integration

- Institutionalizing Restorative Practices: Integrating restorative justice into existing institutional frameworks, policies, and procedures can promote sustainability and long-term impact.

- Continuous Improvement: Implementing regular evaluation and feedback mechanisms allows for continuous improvement and adaptation of restorative programs to meet evolving needs and challenges.

Real-World Examples of Overcoming Challenges

1. New Zealand's Integrated Approach

- Challenge: Resistance to change and resource constraints were significant obstacles to implementing restorative justice.

- Strategy: New Zealand integrated restorative justice into its juvenile justice system through comprehensive training, policy support, and community involvement. The government provided funding and resources to support the transition, resulting in widespread acceptance and successful outcomes.

2. Canada's Victim-Offender Mediation Programs

- Challenge: Ensuring voluntary participation and addressing power imbalances were critical issues.

- Strategy: Canadian VOM programs prioritized informed consent and created safe, supportive environments for participants. Facilitators received extensive training in managing power dynamics and providing emotional support, leading to high levels of satisfaction and reduced recidivism rates.

3. South Africa's Truth and Reconciliation Commission (TRC)

- Challenge: Cultural sensitivity and creating a safe environment were essential for addressing the deep trauma of apartheid.

- Strategy: The TRC involved community leaders and integrated cultural practices into the restorative process. Trauma-informed approaches and emotional support services were provided, facilitating healing and reconciliation.

Conclusion

Implementing restorative justice presents several challenges, but with thoughtful strategies and committed efforts, these obstacles can be overcome. Building awareness and support, securing resources, ensuring voluntary and equitable participation, creating safe and culturally sensitive environments, and promoting sustainability are crucial steps in this journey. The real-world examples demonstrate that restorative justice can effectively transform justice systems, promote healing, and foster social cohesion. In the chapters that follow, we will continue to explore the transformative potential of restorative justice and its impact on creating a more just and compassionate society.

Criticisms and Controversies: Addressing Criticisms and Debating Contentious Issues

Restorative justice, despite its many benefits, faces a range of criticisms and controversies. These challenges arise from differing perspectives on justice, the effectiveness of restorative practices, and the implementation of these methods within existing legal frameworks. This chapter explores the major criticisms and contentious issues associated with restorative justice, offering a balanced view and addressing these concerns with evidence and arguments.

Major Criticisms of Restorative Justice

1. Perceived Leniency

- Criticism: One of the primary criticisms of restorative justice is that it is perceived as too lenient on offenders. Critics argue that restorative practices may not provide sufficient deterrence or punishment for serious crimes, potentially undermining public confidence in the justice system.

- Response: Restorative justice is not about avoiding consequences but about meaningful accountability. It focuses on offenders taking responsibility, making amends, and engaging in rehabilitative actions, which can be more effective in reducing recidivism than punitive measures. Studies have shown that restorative justice can lead to lower reoffending rates and better outcomes for both victims and offenders.

2. Inconsistent Outcomes

- Criticism: Critics argue that restorative justice can lead to inconsistent outcomes, as the process relies heavily on the discretion of facilitators and the willingness of participants. This variability can result in perceived injustices or unequal treatment.

- Response: While variability exists, restorative justice processes are designed to be flexible and responsive to the needs of the individuals involved. Establishing clear guidelines, training facilitators, and monitoring practices can help ensure consistency and fairness. The personalized nature of restorative justice allows for more tailored and effective resolutions.

3. Victim Participation and Coercion

- Criticism: There are concerns that victims may feel pressured to participate in restorative justice processes, which could re-traumatize them or compromise their autonomy. Critics worry about the potential for coercion, especially in cases involving power imbalances.

- Response: Ensuring voluntary participation and providing comprehensive support for victims are essential. Facilitators must be trained to recognize and mitigate power imbalances, and victims should have access to advocacy and counseling services. Proper safeguards and ethical standards can protect victims' rights and well-being.

4. Suitability for Severe Crimes

- Criticism: Restorative justice is sometimes criticized for being inappropriate for severe crimes, such as sexual assault, domestic violence, or homicide. Critics argue that these offenses require a more formal legal response and that restorative practices may not provide adequate justice or protection for victims.

- Response: While restorative justice may not be suitable for all cases, it can be effective in certain severe crimes if implemented with appropriate safeguards. Restorative processes can offer a space for victims to express their experiences and needs, and for offenders to take genuine responsibility. Each case should be carefully assessed to determine the appropriateness of restorative justice.

5. Integration with Formal Justice Systems

- Criticism: Integrating restorative justice with formal justice systems can be challenging, leading to concerns about the coherence and effectiveness of the overall justice system. Critics worry about potential conflicts between restorative and retributive approaches.

- Response: Successful integration requires collaboration between restorative and formal justice systems. Restorative justice can complement traditional approaches by addressing the underlying causes of crime and promoting rehabilitation. Clear policies, communication, and shared goals can enhance coherence and effectiveness.

Debating Contentious Issues

1. Effectiveness in Reducing Recidivism

- Debate: There is ongoing debate about the effectiveness of restorative justice in reducing recidivism compared to traditional punitive measures.

- Evidence: Numerous studies indicate that restorative justice can be more effective in reducing recidivism. For example, a meta-analysis of restorative justice programs found that they typically result in lower reoffending rates. However, the success of these programs depends on proper implementation and support.

2. Balancing Restorative and Retributive Justice

- Debate: Balancing the principles of restorative and retributive justice is a contentious issue. Some argue for a hybrid approach that incorporates elements of both.

- Perspective: A balanced approach can leverage the strengths of both models. Restorative justice addresses the needs of victims and promotes offender rehabilitation, while retributive justice provides a formal structure for serious offenses. Combining these approaches can create a more comprehensive and effective justice system.

3. Restorative Justice in Schools and Workplaces

- Debate: The application of restorative justice in schools and workplaces raises questions about its appropriateness and effectiveness in non-criminal contexts.

- Perspective: Restorative justice can be highly effective in these settings by promoting a positive culture, improving relationships, and addressing conflicts constructively. Successful programs in schools and workplaces demonstrate the versatility and benefits of restorative practices beyond the criminal justice system.

4. Restorative Justice and Cultural Sensitivity

- Debate: Ensuring cultural sensitivity in restorative justice practices is crucial, as cultural differences can influence perceptions of justice and conflict resolution.

- Perspective: Restorative justice must be adapted to fit the cultural context of the communities it serves. Engaging community leaders, incorporating cultural practices, and providing cultural competence training for facilitators can enhance the effectiveness and acceptance of restorative justice.

5. Victim Satisfaction and Restorative Justice

- Debate: While restorative justice aims to prioritize victims' needs, there is debate about its ability to consistently achieve high levels of victim satisfaction.

- Evidence: Research generally shows high levels of victim satisfaction with restorative justice processes, as victims feel heard and involved in the resolution. However, ensuring ongoing support and addressing any concerns throughout the process are vital for maintaining this satisfaction.

Addressing Criticisms and Improving Restorative Practices

1. Enhanced Training and Standards

- Professional Development: Providing comprehensive training for facilitators and practitioners can improve the quality and consistency of restorative justice processes.

- Standards and Guidelines: Establishing clear standards and guidelines can help ensure fairness, transparency, and effectiveness in restorative practices.

2. Ongoing Research and Evaluation

- Continuous Improvement: Conducting ongoing research and evaluation of restorative justice programs can identify strengths, weaknesses, and areas for improvement.

- Evidence-Based Practices: Implementing evidence-based practices and adapting strategies based on research findings can enhance the effectiveness of restorative justice.

3. Community and Stakeholder Engagement

- Building Trust: Engaging community members, victims, offenders, and stakeholders in the design and implementation of restorative justice programs can build trust and support.

- Collaborative Approaches: Collaborative approaches that involve all stakeholders can ensure that restorative justice meets the needs of the community and aligns with broader justice goals.

4. Balancing Restorative and Retributive Approaches

- Integrated Models: Developing integrated models that combine restorative and retributive elements can create a more balanced and comprehensive justice system.

- Policy Support: Advocating for policies that support the integration of restorative justice into formal justice systems can enhance coherence and effectiveness.

5. Ensuring Victim-Centered Approaches

- Victim Support Services: Providing comprehensive support services for victims, including counseling and advocacy, can ensure their needs are met throughout the restorative process.

- Empowerment and Choice: Empowering victims to choose whether to participate and ensuring they have control over the process can enhance their satisfaction and well-being.

Conclusion

Restorative justice faces several criticisms and controversies, but with thoughtful strategies and committed efforts, these challenges can be addressed. By enhancing training, conducting ongoing research, engaging stakeholders, and balancing restorative and retributive approaches, restorative justice can become a more effective and widely accepted model for addressing harm and promoting healing. The next chapters will continue to explore the transformative potential of restorative justice and its impact on creating a more just and compassionate society.

CHAPTER 07

RESTORATIVE JUSTICE AND THE LEGAL SYSTEMS

Integration with Traditional Justice: How Restorative Justice Can Complement Traditional Legal Systems

The integration of restorative justice with traditional legal systems offers a more comprehensive approach to addressing crime and promoting healing. By combining the strengths of both models, the justice system can better serve victims, offenders, and communities. This chapter explores how restorative justice can complement traditional legal systems, the benefits of such integration, and practical strategies for effective implementation.

Understanding the Traditional Legal System

The traditional legal system, often referred to as retributive justice, focuses on punishment and deterrence. It operates on the principles of law enforcement, adjudication, and sentencing, aiming to uphold social order and deter future offenses.

1. Key Characteristics of Traditional Legal Systems

- Retribution and Deterrence: Emphasis on punishing offenders to deter future crimes.

- Adversarial Process: A formal, adversarial process where the state prosecutes offenders, and defense attorneys represent their clients.

- Focus on Guilt and Punishment: Determining guilt and assigning punishment based on established legal standards and procedures.

2. Limitations of Traditional Legal Systems

- Limited Victim Involvement: Victims often have a limited role, leading to feelings of exclusion and dissatisfaction.

- Focus on Punishment: Emphasis on punishment rather than rehabilitation and reparation can result in high recidivism rates and insufficient support for offender reintegration.

- Overburdened Systems: Courts and correctional facilities are often overburdened, leading to delays, overcrowding, and strained resources.

Complementary Role of Restorative Justice

Restorative justice addresses some of the limitations of traditional legal systems by focusing on repairing harm, promoting accountability, and facilitating healing. It complements traditional justice by offering alternative and supplementary approaches to conflict resolution.

1. Key Principles of Restorative Justice

- Repairing Harm: Emphasis on addressing the harm caused by crime and making amends.

- Accountability and Responsibility: Encouraging offenders to take responsibility for their actions and engage in reparative actions.

- Victim and Community Involvement: Actively involving victims and community members in the justice process to promote healing and reconciliation.

2. Benefits of Integrating Restorative Justice with Traditional Legal Systems

- Enhanced Victim Support: Providing victims with a voice and active role in the justice process, leading to higher levels of satisfaction and healing.

- Effective Rehabilitation: Focusing on offender accountability and rehabilitation, reducing recidivism rates and supporting reintegration.

- Resource Efficiency: Alleviating the burden on courts and correctional facilities by offering alternative resolution mechanisms.

- Community Cohesion: Strengthening community bonds and promoting social harmony through collective responsibility and support.

Models of Integration

There are various models for integrating restorative justice with traditional legal systems, each offering different levels of incorporation and collaboration.

1. Pre-Charge Diversion Programs

- Description: Offenders are diverted to restorative justice programs before formal charges are filed, allowing for early intervention and resolution.

- Benefits: Reduces the burden on the court system, provides timely resolution, and offers opportunities for rehabilitation and reparation without a criminal record.

2. Post-Charge but Pre-Sentencing Programs

- Description: Restorative justice processes are initiated after charges are filed but before sentencing. Successful participation can influence sentencing decisions.

- Benefits: Encourages offenders to engage in reparative actions, potentially leading to reduced sentences and better outcomes for victims and offenders.

3. Post-Sentencing Programs

- Description: Restorative justice programs are integrated into the correctional system, allowing offenders to participate in restorative processes during incarceration or as part of their probation or parole conditions.

- Benefits: Supports offender rehabilitation, enhances victim satisfaction and facilitates reintegration into the community.

4. Parallel Systems

- Description: Restorative justice operates alongside the traditional legal system, offering complementary pathways for conflict resolution and harm reparation.

- Benefits: Provides flexibility and choice for victims and offenders, addressing diverse needs and promoting more holistic justice outcomes.

Practical Strategies for Effective Integration

Successful integration of restorative justice with traditional legal systems requires careful planning, collaboration, and support from various stakeholders.

1. Policy and Legislative Support

- Creating Legal Frameworks: Developing policies and legislation that support the implementation of restorative justice practices within the legal system.

- Incentivizing Participation: Offering incentives for participation, such as reduced sentences or expungement of records upon successful completion of restorative programs.

2. Training and Capacity Building

- Training for Legal Professionals: Providing training for judges, prosecutors, defense attorneys, and law enforcement officers on restorative justice principles and practices.

- Building Facilitator Capacity: Training skilled facilitators to conduct restorative processes effectively and ethically.

3. Collaboration and Partnerships

- Engaging Community Organizations: Partnering with community organizations, victim advocacy groups, and restorative justice practitioners to implement and support programs.

- Interagency Collaboration: Facilitating collaboration between criminal justice agencies, social services, and restorative justice programs to ensure coordinated and effective implementation.

4. Monitoring and Evaluation

- Continuous Improvement: Implementing mechanisms for monitoring and evaluating restorative justice programs to assess their effectiveness and identify areas for improvement.

- Data Collection and Analysis: Collecting and analyzing data on program outcomes, including victim satisfaction, recidivism rates, and cost-effectiveness, to inform policy and practice.

Case Studies and Examples

Examining real-world examples of successful integration of restorative justice with traditional legal systems highlights best practices and lessons learned.

1. New Zealand's Family Group Conferencing (FGC)

- Background: New Zealand has successfully integrated Family Group Conferencing into its juvenile justice system, providing a restorative alternative to traditional prosecution.

- Implementation: Offenders, victims, and their families participate in facilitated meetings to discuss the harm and develop a plan for making amends.

- Outcome: FGC has led to high levels of victim satisfaction, reduced recidivism rates, and positive rehabilitation outcomes for young offenders.

2. Canada's Restorative Justice Initiatives

- Background: Canada has implemented various restorative justice programs at different stages of the criminal justice process, including pre-charge diversion and post-sentencing initiatives.

- Implementation: Programs involve victim-offender mediation, community restorative boards, and circles, providing opportunities for reconciliation and reparation.

- Outcome: These initiatives have resulted in lower recidivism rates, increased victim satisfaction, and more effective resource utilization.

3. South Africa's Truth and Reconciliation Commission (TRC)

- Background: The TRC was established to address the atrocities committed during apartheid and promote national healing and reconciliation.

- Implementation: The TRC facilitated public hearings where victims and perpetrators could share their experiences, seek forgiveness, and agree on reparative actions.

- Outcome: The TRC played a crucial role in promoting reconciliation and healing in South Africa, providing a model for integrating restorative justice in post-conflict societies.

Challenges and Considerations

Integrating restorative justice with traditional legal systems presents several challenges and considerations that must be addressed to ensure success.

1. Ensuring Voluntary Participation

- Genuine Consent: Participation in restorative processes must be voluntary. Coercion or pressure to participate can undermine the sincerity and outcomes of the process.

- Informed Decision-Making: Providing clear, accessible information about the process and its potential benefits and risks helps ensure genuine consent.

2. Maintaining Fairness and Consistency

- Equitable Treatment: Ensuring that restorative justice practices are applied equitably and consistently across cases to prevent disparities and biases.

- Clear Guidelines: Establishing clear guidelines and standards for restorative processes to maintain fairness and integrity.

3. Balancing Restorative and Retributive Goals

- Complementary Approaches: Balancing restorative and retributive goals to ensure that justice is served while promoting healing and rehabilitation.

Context-Specific Application: Assessing the appropriateness of restorative justice on a case-by-case basis, considering the severity and context of the offense.

4. Building Public Confidence

- Transparency and Accountability: Ensuring transparency and accountability in the implementation of restorative justice to build public trust and confidence.

- Community Engagement: Engaging the community in restorative justice initiatives to foster understanding and support.

Conclusion

Integrating restorative justice with traditional legal systems offers a comprehensive approach to addressing crime and promoting healing. By combining the strengths of both models, the justice system can better serve victims, offenders, and communities. While challenges exist, careful planning, collaboration, and support can lead to successful integration and more effective justice outcomes. The following chapters will continue to explore the transformative potential of restorative justice and its impact on creating a more just and compassionate society.

Legislative Frameworks: Laws and Policies Supporting Restorative Justice

The development and implementation of legislative frameworks are crucial for the successful integration and sustainability of restorative justice practices within traditional legal systems. This chapter examines the laws and policies that support restorative justice, explores different legislative models, and highlights case studies from various jurisdictions.

Understanding Legislative Frameworks for Restorative Justice

Legislative frameworks for restorative justice establish the legal basis for implementing restorative practices within the justice system. These frameworks provide guidelines, standards, and procedures to ensure consistency, fairness, and effectiveness in restorative justice programs.

1. Key Components of Legislative Frameworks

- Legal Recognition: Formal recognition of restorative justice practices within the legal system.

- Standards and Guidelines: Establishing standards and guidelines for the implementation and operation of restorative justice programs.

- Funding and Resources: Allocating funding and resources to support restorative justice initiatives.

- Training and Professional Development: Providing training and professional development for practitioners and stakeholders.

Monitoring and Evaluation: Implementing mechanisms for monitoring and evaluating the effectiveness of restorative justice programs.

2. Types of Legislative Models

- Stand-Alone Legislation: Specific laws dedicated to establishing and regulating restorative justice practices.

- Amendments to Existing Laws: Incorporating restorative justice provisions into existing criminal justice, juvenile justice, or community justice legislation.

- Policy Directives and Guidelines: Issuing policy directives or guidelines to support the implementation of restorative justice programs without formal legislative changes.

Examples of Legislative Frameworks

1. New Zealand: Children, Young Persons, and Their Families Act 1989

- Overview: New Zealand's legislative framework for restorative justice is rooted in the Children, Young Persons, and Their Families Act 1989, which introduced Family Group Conferencing (FGC) as a key component of the juvenile justice system.

- Key Provisions: The Act mandates the use of FGC for most youth offenses, emphasizing the involvement of families and communities in the decision-making process.

- Impact: The legislation has led to significant reductions in youth offending rates and high levels of victim and family satisfaction.

2. Canada: Youth Criminal Justice Act 2003

- Overview: The Youth Criminal Justice Act (YCJA) of 2003 incorporates restorative justice principles into Canada's juvenile justice system.

- Key Provisions: The YCJA encourages the use of extrajudicial measures, such as diversion and restorative justice programs, to address youth crime. It emphasizes the importance of repairing harm and reintegrating young offenders into the community.

- Impact: The Act has contributed to a decline in youth incarceration rates and promoted the use of restorative justice practices across the country.

3. Australia: Crimes (Restorative Justice) Act 2004 (Australian Capital Territory)

- Overview: The Crimes (Restorative Justice) Act 2004 provides a legislative framework for the use of restorative justice in the Australian Capital Territory (ACT).

- Key Provisions: The Act allows for the referral of both juvenile and adult offenders to restorative justice programs at various stages of the criminal justice process. It outlines procedures for conducting restorative conferences and ensures the protection of participants' rights.

- Impact: The legislation has facilitated the integration of restorative justice into the ACT's criminal justice system, resulting in positive outcomes for victims, offenders, and the community.

4. South Africa: Child Justice Act 2008

- Overview: The Child Justice Act 2008 establishes a separate juvenile justice system in South Africa, incorporating restorative justice principles.

- Key Provisions: The Act provides for diversion programs, including restorative justice measures, for children in conflict with the law. It emphasizes the importance of rehabilitation, reintegration, and the participation of families and communities.

- Impact: The legislation has promoted the use of restorative justice in addressing youth crime and contributed to more effective and humane responses to juvenile offending.

Developing Effective Legislative Frameworks

1. Stakeholder Engagement

- Inclusive Process: Engaging a wide range of stakeholders, including victims, offenders, community members, legal professionals, and restorative justice practitioners, in the development of legislative frameworks.

- Collaborative Approach: Facilitating collaboration between government agencies, non-governmental organizations, and community groups to ensure broad support and input.

2. Comprehensive Guidelines and Standards

- Clear Definitions and Objectives: Defining key terms and objectives of restorative justice within the legislative framework to ensure clarity and consistency.

- Procedural Safeguards: Establishing procedural safeguards to protect the rights and well-being of participants, including informed consent, confidentiality, and the right to legal representation.

3. Funding and Resource Allocation

- Adequate Funding: Allocating sufficient funding to support the implementation and sustainability of restorative justice programs, including training, facilitation, and evaluation.

- Resource Support: Providing resources and support for community-based organizations and restorative justice practitioners to ensure effective program delivery.

4. Training and Professional Development

Capacity Building: Investing in the training and professional development of legal professionals, restorative justice facilitators, and other stakeholders to build capacity and ensure high-quality practice.

- Ongoing Education: Implementing ongoing education and training programs to keep practitioners updated on best practices and emerging trends in restorative justice.

5. Monitoring and Evaluation

- Regular Assessment: Implementing mechanisms for regular monitoring and evaluation of restorative justice programs to assess their effectiveness and identify areas for improvement.

- Data Collection and Analysis: Collecting and analyzing data on program outcomes, including victim satisfaction, recidivism rates, and cost-effectiveness, to inform policy and practice.

Challenges in Developing Legislative Frameworks

1. Resistance to Change

- Cultural and Institutional Resistance: Overcoming resistance to change within the legal system and broader society, particularly among stakeholders accustomed to retributive approaches.

- Building Consensus: Building consensus among diverse stakeholders with differing perspectives on justice and conflict resolution.

2. Balancing Flexibility and Consistency

- Flexibility in Implementation: Ensuring that legislative frameworks provide sufficient flexibility to address the unique needs of different cases and communities.

- Maintaining Consistency: Balancing flexibility with the need for consistency and fairness in the application of restorative justice practices.

3. Ensuring Equity and Access

- Addressing Disparities: Addressing potential disparities in access to restorative justice programs, particularly for marginalized and vulnerable populations.

- Promoting Inclusivity: Promoting inclusivity and cultural sensitivity in the design and implementation of restorative justice programs.

Conclusion

The development of legislative frameworks is essential for the successful integration and sustainability of restorative justice practices within traditional legal systems. By establishing clear guidelines, standards, and procedures, these frameworks can support the effective implementation of restorative justice programs and promote positive outcomes for victims, offenders, and communities. While challenges exist, thoughtful and collaborative approaches can overcome these obstacles and create a more just and compassionate justice system. The following chapters will continue to explore the transformative potential of restorative justice and its impact on creating a more equitable and humane society.

Case Law and Precedents: Notable Legal Cases and Their Implications for Restorative Justice

The evolution of restorative justice within the legal system is significantly shaped by case law and judicial precedents. These legal cases illustrate how courts have interpreted and applied restorative justice principles, influencing future practices and policies. This chapter explores notable legal cases that have set important precedents for restorative justice, analyzing their implications and contributions to the development of restorative justice frameworks.

Understanding Case Law and Precedents

Case law refers to the body of judicial decisions that interpret and apply laws in specific cases. Precedents established by higher courts are binding on lower courts within the same jurisdiction, shaping the application of legal principles and policies.

1. Role of Case Law in Restorative Justice

- Interpretation of Legislation: Courts interpret restorative justice legislation and policies, providing clarity on their application and scope.

- Setting Precedents: Judicial decisions set precedents that influence future cases, guiding the integration and practice of restorative justice.

- Evolving Legal Standards: Case law reflects the evolving standards and practices in restorative justice, contributing to its development and acceptance within the legal system.

Notable Legal Cases in Restorative Justice

1. R v. Gladue (1999) – Canada

- Background: The Supreme Court of Canada decision in R v. Gladue addressed the overrepresentation of Indigenous people in the Canadian criminal justice system and emphasized the need for restorative justice approaches.

- Key Points: The Court held that judges must consider the unique circumstances of Indigenous offenders and prioritize restorative justice principles, such as healing and rehabilitation, over incarceration.

- Implications: This landmark decision led to the development of "Gladue reports" and the increased use of restorative justice practices for Indigenous offenders, influencing sentencing practices across Canada.

2. R v. Proulx (2000) – Canada

- Background: In R v. Proulx, the Supreme Court of Canada clarified the application of conditional sentences, emphasizing the importance of restorative justice principles.

- Key Points: The Court affirmed that conditional sentences should be used to promote restorative justice, focusing on reparation, rehabilitation, and community involvement.

- Implications: This decision reinforced the role of restorative justice in sentencing, encouraging the use of community-based alternatives to incarceration.

3. Mabo v. Queensland (No. 2) (1992) – Australia

- Background: The High Court of Australia's decision in Mabo v. Queensland (No. 2) recognized Indigenous land rights and emphasized the need for restorative justice in addressing historical injustices.

- Key Points: The Court's recognition of native title and the need for reconciliation highlighted the importance of restorative justice principles in legal and social contexts.

- Implications: This decision paved the way for greater integration of restorative justice approaches in addressing Indigenous rights and reconciliation efforts in Australia.

4. South Africa's Truth and Reconciliation Commission (TRC) – Post-Apartheid Era

- Background: The TRC was established to address the atrocities committed during apartheid in South Africa, using restorative justice principles to promote healing and reconciliation.

- Key Points: The TRC facilitated public hearings where victims and perpetrators could share their experiences, seek forgiveness, and agree on reparative actions.

- Implications: The TRC's work set a global precedent for using restorative justice in post-conflict societies, demonstrating its potential to address systemic injustices and promote national healing.

5. R v. Restorative Justice Tribunal (Fictional Example) – United Kingdom

- Background: A hypothetical case involving the establishment of a Restorative Justice Tribunal to handle certain criminal cases in the UK.

- Key Points: The Tribunal focuses on restorative practices, including victim-offender mediation and community restitution, as part of its adjudication process.

- Implications: This example illustrates how specialized restorative justice bodies can complement traditional courts, offering alternative pathways for conflict resolution and harm reparation.

Analysis of Legal Precedents

1. Promoting Restorative Principles in Sentencing

- Sentencing Guidelines: Judicial decisions that emphasize restorative justice principles in sentencing guidelines encourage the use of non-custodial measures and reparative actions.

- Rehabilitation and Reintegration: Precedents that prioritize rehabilitation and community reintegration over punitive measures support the development of more humane and effective justice practices.

2. Addressing Systemic Injustices

- Indigenous Rights and Reconciliation: Cases like R v. Gladue and Mabo v. Queensland (No. 2) highlight the role of restorative justice in addressing historical and systemic injustices, promoting reconciliation and social equity.

- Post-Conflict Societies: The TRC's work in South Africa demonstrates the potential of restorative justice to facilitate healing and reconciliation in post-conflict societies, providing a model for other nations.

3. Enhancing Victim Participation and Satisfaction

- Victim-Centered Approaches: Judicial decisions that prioritize victim participation and satisfaction in restorative processes contribute to higher levels of victim empowerment and emotional healing.

- Reparative Actions: Encouraging reparative actions and community involvement in sentencing and dispute resolution promotes a more holistic approach to justice.

Challenges and Considerations

1. Consistency in Application

- Ensuring Uniformity: Ensuring uniform application of restorative justice principles across different jurisdictions and cases is a challenge, requiring clear guidelines and ongoing training for legal professionals.

- Balancing Flexibility and Fairness: Balancing the flexibility of restorative practices with the need for consistent and fair outcomes is essential to maintaining public trust and confidence in the justice system.

2. Integrating Restorative Justice with Formal Legal Systems

- Legal and Institutional Resistance: Overcoming resistance within traditional legal systems and institutions is necessary for the successful integration of restorative justice practices.

- Collaborative Approaches: Developing collaborative approaches that involve legal professionals, restorative justice practitioners, and community members can enhance the integration and effectiveness of restorative justice.

3. Protecting Participants' Rights

- Voluntary Participation: Ensuring that participation in restorative justice processes is voluntary and informed is critical to protecting the rights and well-being of participants.

- Addressing Power Imbalances: Recognizing and addressing power imbalances between victims and offenders is essential to ensuring equitable and just outcomes.

Conclusion

Notable legal cases and judicial precedents have played a significant role in shaping the integration and practice of restorative justice within traditional legal systems. By promoting restorative principles in sentencing, addressing systemic injustices, and enhancing victim participation, these decisions contribute to the development of more holistic and effective justice practices. While challenges remain, ongoing efforts to address these issues and build on successful precedents can further advance the transformative potential of restorative justice. The following chapters will continue to explore the impact of restorative justice on creating a more just and compassionate society.

CHAPTER 08

RESTORATIVE JUSTICE IN THE INTERNATIONAL CONTEXT

Global Perspectives: Restorative Justice Practices Around the World

Restorative justice has gained traction worldwide as an effective and humane approach to addressing crime and conflict. This chapter explores the diverse ways in which restorative justice is practiced globally, highlighting regional approaches, cultural adaptations, and the impact of these practices on various communities. By examining restorative justice in different international contexts, we can gain a deeper understanding of its universal principles and its adaptability to local needs and traditions.

Restorative Justice in North America

1. Canada

- Indigenous Restorative Practices: Canada has a rich history of Indigenous restorative justice practices, such as the Cree concept of "healing circles" and the Navajo "peacemaking" process. These traditional practices have influenced modern restorative justice programs across the country.

- Youth Criminal Justice Act (YCJA): The YCJA promotes the use of restorative justice for young offenders, emphasizing diversion programs, community service, and victim-offender mediation.

- Community-Based Programs: Canada has numerous community-based restorative justice programs that address a wide range of offenses, focusing on rehabilitation and community involvement.

2. United States

- Juvenile Justice Reform: Several states have integrated restorative justice into their juvenile justice systems, using practices such as victim-offender dialogues, family group conferencing, and restorative circles.

- School-Based Programs: Restorative justice is increasingly being implemented in schools across the United States to address bullying, reduce suspensions, and create positive school climates.

- Community Restorative Boards: Some communities use restorative boards composed of trained volunteers to address minor offenses and support offender reintegration.

Restorative Justice in Europe

1. United Kingdom

- Restorative Justice Council: The UK has established the Restorative Justice Council to promote and regulate restorative practices. The Council provides training, accreditation, and resources to ensure high standards in restorative justice delivery.

- Criminal Justice System Integration: Restorative justice is integrated into the UK's criminal justice system, with practices such as restorative conferencing and victim-offender mediation used at various stages of the justice process.

- Education Sector: Many schools in the UK have adopted restorative approaches to manage behavior, resolve conflicts, and improve school climates.

2. Norway

- Conflict Resolution Boards: Norway has implemented conflict resolution boards, known as "konfliktråd," which handle minor offenses and disputes through restorative practices. These boards involve community members and focus on dialogue and reparation.

- Juvenile Justice: Restorative justice is a key component of Norway's juvenile justice system, emphasizing rehabilitation and reintegration over punishment.

3. Germany

- Victim-Offender Mediation: Germany has a well-established system of victim-offender mediation, known as "Täter-Opfer-Ausgleich," which is used for both juvenile and adult offenders. The process aims to repair harm, promote understanding, and achieve mutually agreeable outcomes.

- Community-Based Programs: Various community-based restorative justice programs in Germany address different types of offenses, focusing on victim support and offender accountability.

Restorative Justice in Africa

1. South Africa

- Truth and Reconciliation Commission (TRC): The TRC is a landmark example of restorative justice in a post-conflict society. It facilitated public hearings where victims and perpetrators of apartheid-era atrocities could share their experiences and seek reconciliation.

- Community Restorative Programs: South Africa has implemented numerous community-based restorative justice programs that address local conflicts and promote social cohesion.

2. Kenya

- Traditional Justice Systems: Kenya's traditional justice systems, such as the "Elders' Councils," incorporate restorative principles to resolve disputes and promote community harmony.

- Formal Integration: Efforts are being made to integrate restorative justice into the formal legal system, particularly for juvenile offenders and minor offenses.

Restorative Justice in Asia

1. New Zealand

- Family Group Conferencing (FGC): New Zealand is a pioneer in the use of FGC, which is mandated for juvenile offenders under the Children, Young Persons, and Their Families Act 1989. FGC involves families, victims, and community members in the decision-making process.

- Indigenous Practices: Maori concepts of justice, such as "whānau" (family) and "hapū" (sub-tribe), emphasize collective responsibility and restorative principles, influencing mainstream restorative practices.

2. Japan

- Reconciliation Committees: Japan's legal system incorporates reconciliation committees that facilitate mediation between victims and offenders, promoting resolution and reparation.

\- Community Involvement: Community involvement is a key aspect of restorative justice in Japan, with local volunteers often participating in the reconciliation process.

3. Singapore

\- Juvenile Justice System: Singapore has integrated restorative justice into its juvenile justice system, focusing on rehabilitation and reintegration. Practices such as family group conferencing and victim-offender mediation are commonly used.

Restorative Justice in Latin America

1. Brazil

\- Restorative Circles: Brazil has implemented restorative circles in various contexts, including schools, prisons, and community settings, to address conflicts and promote healing.

\- Community-Based Initiatives: Community-based restorative justice initiatives in Brazil focus on addressing local conflicts and building stronger, more cohesive communities.

2. Argentina

- Juvenile Justice Reform: Argentina has incorporated restorative justice principles into its juvenile justice system, emphasizing diversion, rehabilitation, and community involvement.

- Victim-Offender Mediation: Programs such as victim-offender mediation are used to resolve conflicts and support victim healing.

Cultural Adaptations and Challenges

1. Cultural Sensitivity and Relevance

- Adapting Practices: Restorative justice practices must be adapted to fit the cultural context of the communities they serve. This includes respecting local customs, traditions, and values.

- Engaging Local Leaders: Engaging local leaders and community members in the design and implementation of restorative justice programs can enhance their cultural relevance and acceptance.

2. Addressing Power Imbalances

- Equitable Participation: Ensuring equitable participation and addressing power imbalances between victims and offenders is crucial for effective restorative justice.

- Providing Support: Offering support services, such as counseling and advocacy, can help vulnerable participants engage more fully in the restorative process.

3. Ensuring Sustainability

- Funding and Resources: Securing funding and resources is essential for the sustainability of restorative justice programs. Governments, NGOs, and international organizations can play a role in providing financial support.

- Training and Capacity Building: Investing in training and capacity building for practitioners and community members ensures the effective implementation and sustainability of restorative practices.

Conclusion

Restorative justice practices have been adopted and adapted in various international contexts, demonstrating their universal appeal and effectiveness in addressing harm, promoting healing, and fostering social cohesion. By examining global perspectives on restorative justice, we can appreciate the diverse ways in which these principles are applied and the positive impact they have on communities worldwide. The following chapters will continue to explore the transformative potential of restorative justice and its impact on creating a more just and compassionate society.

Restorative Justice in International Contexts

Transitional Justice: Restorative Approaches in Post-Conflict and Transitional Societies

Transitional justice refers to the ways societies address legacies of mass violence, human rights abuses, and systemic injustices during periods of political transition, such as post-conflict or post-authoritarian regimes. Restorative approaches within transitional justice aim to heal communities, promote reconciliation, and build a foundation for sustainable peace. This chapter explores how restorative justice is implemented in transitional societies, highlighting key principles, mechanisms, and case studies.

Understanding Transitional Justice

Transitional justice encompasses a range of judicial and non-judicial measures designed to address past atrocities and promote healing and reconciliation. These measures include truth commissions, reparations, institutional reforms, and criminal prosecutions.

1. Key Principles of Transitional Justice

- Truth and Acknowledgment: Establishing an accurate historical record of past abuses and ensuring public acknowledgment of the truth.

- Justice and Accountability: Holding perpetrators accountable through legal and restorative processes.

- Reparation and Redress: Providing reparations to victims, including material compensation, symbolic gestures, and community rebuilding.

- Reconciliation and Healing: Promoting reconciliation between conflicting parties and fostering societal healing.

2. Restorative Justice in Transitional Contexts

- Restorative justice focuses on repairing harm, promoting accountability, and fostering reconciliation. In transitional societies, restorative approaches can address the needs of victims, reintegrate perpetrators, and rebuild trust within communities.

Mechanisms of Restorative Transitional Justice

1. Truth Commissions

- Purpose: Truth commissions investigate and document past human rights violations, providing a platform for victims and perpetrators to share their experiences.

- Restorative Elements: These commissions often incorporate restorative elements, such as public hearings, victim testimonies, and recommendations for reparations and reconciliation.

2. Community-Based Restorative Practices

- Purpose: Community-based practices involve local communities in resolving conflicts and addressing past harms through dialogue, mediation, and collective decision-making.

- Restorative Elements: These practices emphasize participation, empowerment, and community healing, fostering a sense of collective responsibility and solidarity.

3. Victim-Offender Mediation and Dialogues

- Purpose: Facilitated dialogues between victims and perpetrators aim to address the harm, promote understanding, and develop reparative actions.

- Restorative Elements: These processes encourage accountability, empathy, and mutual recognition, contributing to personal and societal healing.

4. Reparations Programs

- Purpose: Reparations programs provide compensation and support to victims of human rights abuses, recognizing their suffering and contributing to their recovery.

- Restorative Elements: Reparations can include financial compensation, healthcare, education, and symbolic measures, such as apologies and memorials.

5. Institutional Reforms

- Purpose: Institutional reforms aim to address the root causes of conflict and prevent future abuses by transforming justice, security, and governance systems.

- Restorative Elements: Reforms emphasize accountability, transparency, and the inclusion of marginalized groups, promoting a more just and equitable society.

Case Studies of Restorative Transitional Justice

1. South Africa: Truth and Reconciliation Commission (TRC)

- Background: Established in 1995, the TRC addressed the atrocities committed during apartheid, promoting national healing and reconciliation.

- Mechanisms: The TRC held public hearings where victims and perpetrators shared their experiences. It provided amnesty to perpetrators who fully disclosed their actions and recommended reparations for victims.

- Outcomes: The TRC contributed to a national acknowledgment of past abuses, promoted forgiveness and reconciliation, and set a precedent for restorative justice in post conflict societies.

2. Rwanda: Gacaca Courts

- Background: Following the 1994 genocide, Rwanda established the Gacaca courts to address the massive backlog of genocide-related cases and promote community healing.

- Mechanisms: Gacaca courts were community-based tribunals that relied on local participation and restorative principles to adjudicate cases, emphasizing truth-telling, accountability, and reparation.

- Outcomes: The Gacaca courts resolved a significant number of cases, facilitated local reconciliation, and promoted a sense of justice and closure for many victims and communities.

3. Colombia: Special Jurisdiction for Peace (JEP)

- Background: As part of the 2016 peace agreement between the Colombian government and the FARC guerrillas, the JEP was established to address crimes committed during the armed conflict.

- Mechanisms: The JEP incorporates restorative justice principles, allowing perpetrators to receive reduced sentences in exchange for truth-telling, reparations, and contributions to community rebuilding.

- Outcomes: The JEP aims to promote accountability, support victims, and foster reconciliation, contributing to Colombia's broader peacebuilding efforts.

4. Sierra Leone: Truth and Reconciliation Commission (TRC)

- Background: Sierra Leone's TRC was established after the civil war to investigate human rights violations, promote reconciliation, and recommend reparations.

- Mechanisms: The TRC held public hearings, gathered testimonies, and emphasized community involvement in the reconciliation process.

- Outcomes: The TRC's work contributed to a deeper understanding of the conflict's impact, supported victim healing, and provided a foundation for ongoing peacebuilding.

Challenges and Considerations

1. Balancing Justice and Reconciliation

- Challenge: Balancing the need for justice and accountability with the goals of reconciliation and healing can be challenging, particularly in contexts of widespread and severe abuses.

- Consideration: Integrating both retributive and restorative elements, and ensuring that victims' needs and rights are prioritized, can help achieve a balanced approach.

2. Ensuring Inclusivity and Participation

- Challenge: Ensuring the meaningful participation of all stakeholders, including marginalized and vulnerable groups, is essential for the legitimacy and effectiveness of restorative transitional justice.

- Consideration: Engaging local communities, civil society organizations, and affected populations in the design and implementation of restorative processes can enhance inclusivity and ownership.

3. Managing Expectations and Outcomes

- Challenge: Managing the diverse and often high expectations of victims, perpetrators, and communities can be complex, particularly in volatile and rapidly changing environments.

- Consideration: Setting realistic goals, communicating transparently, and being responsive to evolving needs and contexts can help manage expectations and achieve sustainable outcomes.

4. Sustaining Long-Term Impact

- Challenge: Ensuring the long-term sustainability of restorative justice initiatives in transitional contexts requires ongoing commitment, resources, and institutional support.

- Consideration: Building local capacity, securing financial and political support, and integrating restorative practices into broader peacebuilding and development strategies can support sustainability.

Conclusion

Restorative justice plays a critical role in transitional justice, offering effective and humane approaches to addressing past atrocities, promoting healing, and building sustainable peace. By examining case studies from diverse contexts, we can appreciate the adaptability and impact of restorative practices in post-conflict and transitional societies. While challenges exist, thoughtful and inclusive approaches can enhance the effectiveness and sustainability of restorative justice, contributing to more just and reconciled communities. The following chapters will continue to explore the transformative potential of restorative justice and its impact on creating a more just and compassionate society.

Human Rights and Restorative Justice: The Relationship Between Human Rights and Restorative Practices

Restorative justice and human rights share a common foundation in promoting dignity, respect, and justice for all individuals. The relationship between these two fields is crucial in ensuring that restorative practices uphold and advance human rights principles. This chapter explores the intersection of human rights and restorative justice, examining how restorative practices can support human rights, the challenges involved, and real-world examples of their integration.

Understanding the Relationship Between Human Rights and Restorative Justice

1. Common Principles

- Dignity and Respect: Both human rights and restorative justice emphasize the inherent dignity and respect due to every individual, regardless of their actions or status.

- Accountability and Justice: Both frameworks seek accountability and justice, aiming to repair harm and ensure that wrongdoers take responsibility for their actions.

- Participation and Inclusion: Both prioritize the participation and inclusion of all affected parties, ensuring that voices are heard and respected in the pursuit of justice.

2. Complementary Goals

- Promoting Healing and Reparation: Restorative justice focuses on healing and reparation, aligning with human rights principles that seek to address and remedy violations.

- Preventing Future Harm: By addressing the root causes of conflict and harm, restorative justice contributes to the prevention of future human rights violations.

- Empowering Victims: Restorative practices empower victims by giving them a voice and active role in the justice process, aligning with human rights principles of victim-centered justice.

How Restorative Justice Supports Human Rights

1. Addressing Human Rights Violations

- Truth and Reconciliation Commissions: These commissions investigate and document human rights violations, providing a platform for victims and perpetrators to share their experiences and seek reconciliation. They help establish an accurate historical record and promote healing and justice.

- Community-Based Restorative Practices: In communities affected by human rights abuses, restorative practices can facilitate dialogue, understanding, and collective healing, addressing the harm and promoting social cohesion.

2. Rehabilitation and Reintegration of Offenders

- Restorative Justice Programs: These programs focus on the rehabilitation and reintegration of offenders, ensuring that they take responsibility for their actions and make amends to victims and communities. This approach aligns with human rights principles that emphasize the potential for rehabilitation and the humane treatment of offenders.

3. Empowering Marginalized Groups

- Inclusive Practices: Restorative justice practices can be designed to include and empower marginalized groups, ensuring that their voices are heard and their rights are respected. This approach helps address systemic inequalities and promote social justice.

4. Reparations and Redress

- Reparative Measures: Restorative justice emphasizes reparative measures, such as apologies, compensation, and community service, to address harm and support victims. These measures align with human rights principles that call for effective remedies for victims of violations.

Challenges in Integrating Human Rights and Restorative Justice

1. Balancing Rights and Accountability

- Ensuring Accountability: Ensuring that restorative justice processes hold perpetrators accountable while respecting their rights can be challenging. It requires careful design and implementation to balance these objectives.

- Voluntary Participation: Ensuring that participation in restorative processes is voluntary and informed is crucial to protecting the rights and dignity of all participants.

2. Addressing Power Imbalances

- Equitable Participation: Power imbalances between victims and offenders can affect the fairness and effectiveness of restorative processes. Facilitators must be skilled in recognizing and addressing these imbalances to ensure equitable participation.

- Support Services: Providing support services, such as counseling and advocacy, can help vulnerable participants engage fully in the restorative process.

3. Cultural Sensitivity and Context

- Adapting Practices: Restorative justice practices must be adapted to fit the cultural context and respect local customs and traditions. This adaptation helps ensure that practices are relevant and effective while upholding human rights principles.

- Engaging Communities: Engaging local communities in the design and implementation of restorative justice programs enhances their cultural sensitivity and acceptance.

4. Sustainability and Resources

- Securing Funding: Ensuring adequate funding and resources for restorative justice programs is essential for their sustainability and effectiveness.

- Training and Capacity Building: Investing in training and capacity building for practitioners and community members ensures high-quality and consistent practice.

Real-World Examples of Integration

1. South Africa: Truth and Reconciliation Commission (TRC)

   - Human Rights Focus: The TRC was established to address the gross human rights violations committed during apartheid. It aimed to promote national healing and reconciliation through restorative justice principles.

   - Mechanisms: The TRC held public hearings where victims and perpetrators shared their experiences. It provided amnesty to perpetrators who fully disclosed their actions and recommended reparations for victims.

   - Outcomes: The TRC contributed to a national acknowledgment of past abuses, promoted forgiveness and reconciliation, and set a precedent for integrating human rights and restorative justice.

2. Canada: Indigenous Restorative Justice Programs

   - Human Rights Focus: Canada has implemented restorative justice programs that incorporate Indigenous practices, addressing the historical injustices and human rights violations faced by Indigenous communities.

   - Mechanisms: Programs such as healing circles and peacemaking processes involve victims, offenders, and community members in dialogue and collective decision-making.

- Outcomes: These programs promote healing, reconciliation, and the empowerment of Indigenous communities, aligning with human rights principles.

3. Rwanda: Gacaca Courts

- Human Rights Focus: Following the 1994 genocide, Rwanda established the Gacaca courts to address the massive backlog of genocide-related cases and promote community healing.

- Mechanisms: Gacaca courts were community-based tribunals that relied on local participation and restorative principles to adjudicate cases, emphasizing truth-telling, accountability, and reparation.

- Outcomes: The Gacaca courts resolved a significant number of cases, facilitated local reconciliation, and promoted a sense of justice and closure for many victims and communities.

4. Colombia: Special Jurisdiction for Peace (JEP)

- Human Rights Focus: As part of the 2016 peace agreement between the Colombian government and the FARC guerrillas, the JEP was established to address crimes committed during the armed conflict.

- Mechanisms: The JEP incorporates restorative justice principles, allowing perpetrators to receive reduced sentences in exchange for truth-telling, reparations, and contributions to community rebuilding.

- Outcomes: The JEP aims to promote accountability, support victims, and foster reconciliation, contributing to Colombia's broader peacebuilding efforts.

Strategies for Effective Integration

1. Policy and Legislative Support

- Creating Legal Frameworks: Developing policies and legislation that support the integration of restorative justice and human rights principles.

- Incentivizing Participation: Offering incentives for participation, such as reduced sentences or expungement of records upon successful completion of restorative programs.

2. Training and Capacity Building

- Training for Practitioners: Providing comprehensive training for restorative justice practitioners on human rights principles and practices.

- Building Community Capacity: Investing in capacity building for community members to enhance their understanding of restorative justice and human rights.

3. Collaboration and Partnerships

- Engaging Stakeholders: Collaborating with human rights organizations, legal professionals, and community groups to ensure the effective integration of restorative justice and human rights.

- Interagency Collaboration: Facilitating collaboration between criminal justice agencies, human rights bodies, and restorative justice programs to ensure coordinated and effective implementation.

4. Monitoring and Evaluation

- Continuous Improvement: Implementing mechanisms for monitoring and evaluating restorative justice programs to assess their effectiveness and identify areas for improvement.

- Data Collection and Analysis: Collecting and analyzing data on program outcomes, including victim satisfaction, recidivism rates, and human rights impacts, to inform policy and practice.

Conclusion

The relationship between human rights and restorative justice is fundamental to promoting dignity, respect, and justice for all individuals. By integrating human rights principles into restorative practices, we can ensure that these approaches uphold and advance the rights of victims, offenders, and communities. Real-world examples demonstrate the positive impact of this integration, highlighting the potential for restorative justice to address human rights violations, promote healing, and build more just and equitable societies. The following chapters will continue to explore the transformative potential of restorative justice and its impact on creating a more just and compassionate world.

CHAPTER 09

RESTORATIVE JUSTICE AND SOCIAL JUSTICE

Intersectionality: Addressing Issues of Race, Gender, and Class in Restorative Justice

Intersectionality is a critical framework for understanding how multiple social identities, such as race, gender, and class, intersect to create unique experiences of privilege and oppression. Applying an intersectional lens to restorative justice is essential for addressing the complex and interconnected forms of discrimination and inequality that individuals face. This chapter explores the importance of intersectionality in restorative justice, examines how it influences the experiences of participants, and offers strategies for implementing intersectional restorative practices.

Understanding Intersectionality

1. Definition and Origins

- Concept: Intersectionality is a framework developed by Kimberlé Crenshaw to describe how different social identities, such as race, gender, and class, intersect and interact to produce unique experiences of marginalization or privilege.

- Importance: It highlights the interconnected nature of social categorizations and the need to consider multiple dimensions of identity in understanding social inequality and injustice.

2. Relevance to Restorative Justice

- Holistic Approach: Restorative justice aims to address harm, promote healing, and restore relationships. Incorporating intersectionality ensures that these goals are achieved in a way that acknowledges and addresses the complex realities of participants' lives.

- Equity and Inclusion: An intersectional approach promotes equity and inclusion by recognizing and addressing the specific needs and challenges faced by individuals based on their intersecting identities.

Intersectionality in Restorative Justice Practices

1. Race and Ethnicity

- Racial Disparities: Racial and ethnic minorities often face systemic discrimination and overrepresentation in the criminal justice system. Restorative justice must address these disparities to promote fairness and justice.

- Culturally Relevant Practices: Incorporating culturally relevant practices and perspectives into restorative justice processes can enhance their effectiveness and ensure they resonate with participants from diverse racial and ethnic backgrounds.

2. Gender

- Gender-Based Violence: Restorative justice can be a valuable tool for addressing gender-based violence, such as domestic violence and sexual assault, by focusing on healing, accountability, and empowerment.

- Gender Sensitivity: Ensuring gender sensitivity in restorative processes involves recognizing and addressing the unique experiences and needs of individuals based on their gender identities.

3. Class and Socioeconomic Status

- Economic Inequality: Economic inequality can influence individuals' access to justice and their experiences within the justice system. Restorative justice must consider these economic factors to promote fairness and equity.

- Resource Allocation: Ensuring that restorative justice programs are accessible to individuals from all socioeconomic backgrounds requires addressing barriers such as cost, availability, and support services.

Case Studies and Examples

1. Race and Restorative Justice in the United States

- Background: The United States has a long history of racial disparities in the criminal justice system, with African Americans and other racial minorities disproportionately affected.

- Restorative Approaches: Programs like the Restorative Community Conferencing (RCC) in Oakland, California, address racial disparities by involving community members in the justice process and focusing on culturally relevant practices.

- Outcomes: RCC has demonstrated success in reducing recidivism rates and improving outcomes for youth of color, highlighting the importance of addressing racial disparities through restorative justice.

2. Gender and Restorative Justice in Canada

- Background: Canada has implemented restorative justice programs to address gender-based violence, such as domestic violence and sexual assault.

- Restorative Approaches: Programs like the Community Holistic Circle Healing (CHCH) in Hollow Water

First Nation focus on healing, accountability, and community involvement, incorporating Indigenous cultural practices.

- Outcomes: CHCH has shown success in reducing reoffending rates and promoting healing for survivors of gender-based violence, demonstrating the effectiveness of gender-sensitive restorative justice practices.

3. Class and Restorative Justice in the United Kingdom

- Background: Socioeconomic inequality in the United Kingdom affects individuals' access to justice and their experiences within the justice system.

- Restorative Approaches: Programs like the Bristol Restorative Justice Service focus on making restorative justice accessible to individuals from all socioeconomic backgrounds by providing free services and support.

- Outcomes: These programs have improved access to justice for economically disadvantaged individuals and promoted more equitable outcomes, emphasizing the importance of addressing class in restorative justice.

Strategies for Implementing Intersectional Restorative Practices

1. Training and Capacity Building

- Intersectional Awareness: Providing training for restorative justice practitioners on intersectionality and its relevance to justice practices can enhance their ability to recognize and address the complex identities of participants.

- Cultural Competence: Building cultural competence among practitioners ensures that restorative justice processes are respectful, relevant, and effective for participants from diverse backgrounds.

2. Inclusive and Participatory Processes

- Engaging Communities: Involving community members and leaders in the design and implementation of restorative justice programs can ensure that these programs reflect the diverse needs and perspectives of the community.

- Participant-Centered Approach: Adopting a participant-centered approach that prioritizes the voices and experiences of those affected by harm promotes inclusivity and empowerment.

3. Addressing Systemic Inequality

- Policy Advocacy: Advocating for policies that address systemic inequalities and promote equity within the justice system can support the integration of intersectional restorative practices.

- Resource Allocation: Ensuring adequate funding and resources for restorative justice programs, particularly those serving marginalized and disadvantaged communities, is essential for promoting equity and inclusion.

4. Monitoring and Evaluation

- Data Collection: Collecting data on participants' demographic characteristics and experiences can help identify disparities and inform the development of more equitable restorative justice practices.

- Continuous Improvement: Implementing mechanisms for ongoing monitoring and evaluation ensures that restorative justice programs are responsive to the needs of participants and continuously improve in promoting equity and justice.

Challenges and Considerations

1. Navigating Power Dynamics

- Recognizing Power Imbalances: Identifying and addressing power imbalances between participants, such as those based on race, gender, or class, is essential for ensuring fairness and effectiveness in restorative justice processes.

- Providing Support: Offering support services, such as advocacy and counseling, can help mitigate power imbalances and empower participants.

2. Ensuring Voluntary Participation

- Informed Consent: Ensuring that participation in restorative justice processes is voluntary and based on informed consent is critical for respecting participants' autonomy and dignity.

- Creating Safe Spaces: Establishing safe and supportive environments where participants feel comfortable sharing their experiences and engaging in dialogue is essential for effective restorative justice.

3. Balancing Individual and Collective Needs

- Individual Healing and Collective Justice: Balancing the needs of individual participants with the broader goals of collective healing and social justice can be challenging. It requires a nuanced and flexible approach that considers the unique circumstances of each case.

Conclusion

Applying an intersectional lens to restorative justice is essential for addressing the complex and interconnected forms of discrimination and inequality that individuals face. By recognizing and addressing the unique experiences of participants based on their intersecting identities, restorative justice can promote equity, inclusion, and social justice. Real-world examples demonstrate the importance and effectiveness of intersectional restorative practices, highlighting the potential for these approaches to create more just and compassionate communities. The following chapters will continue to explore the transformative potential of restorative justice and its impact on creating a more just and equitable society.

Social Equity: Promoting Fairness and Equality Through Restorative Practices

Social equity is the pursuit of fairness and justice in the distribution of resources, opportunities, and treatment across all societal groups. Restorative justice offers a powerful framework for promoting social equity by addressing harms, fostering accountability, and emphasizing the restoration of relationships and communities. This chapter explores the role of restorative practices in advancing social equity, discussing key principles, challenges, strategies, and case studies that highlight successful integration.

Understanding Social Equity

1. Definition and Importance

- Social Equity: Social equity involves ensuring that all individuals have fair access to resources, opportunities, and treatment, regardless of their social, economic, or demographic characteristics.

- Importance: Promoting social equity is essential for creating just and inclusive societies where everyone can achieve their full potential and contribute to the common good.

2. Restorative Justice and Social Equity

- Alignment of Goals: Restorative justice aligns with social equity by addressing the underlying causes of harm, promoting healing and reparation, and fostering inclusive and participatory processes.

- Focus on Marginalized Groups: Restorative practices can be particularly effective in addressing the needs and rights of marginalized and disadvantaged groups, promoting their inclusion and empowerment.

Principles of Social Equity in Restorative Justice

1. Fairness and Justice

- Equitable Treatment: Ensuring that all individuals are treated fairly and justly within restorative processes, regardless of their background or circumstances.

- Addressing Disparities: Actively addressing disparities and inequalities that may exist within the justice system and society at large.

2. Participation and Inclusion

- Inclusive Processes: Designing restorative processes that are inclusive and accessible to all individuals, particularly those from marginalized or disadvantaged groups.

- Empowering Participants: Empowering participants by giving them a voice and active role in the justice process, promoting their agency and self-determination.

3. Accountability and Reparation

- Holding Offenders Accountable: Ensuring that offenders take responsibility for their actions and make meaningful amends to those harmed.

- Supporting Victims: Providing comprehensive support to victims, including opportunities for healing, reparation, and empowerment.

Challenges in Promoting Social Equity Through Restorative Practices

1. Systemic Inequality and Bias

- Recognizing Bias: Acknowledging and addressing systemic inequalities and biases that may influence restorative justice processes and outcomes.

- Mitigating Disparities: Implementing measures to mitigate disparities and ensure equitable treatment for all participants.

2. Resource Allocation and Accessibility

- Ensuring Accessibility: Ensuring that restorative justice programs are accessible to all individuals, regardless of their socioeconomic status, location, or other barriers.

- Adequate Funding: Securing adequate funding and resources to support restorative justice initiatives and ensure their sustainability and effectiveness.

3. Cultural Sensitivity and Relevance

- Adapting Practices: Adapting restorative practices to fit the cultural contexts and needs of diverse communities, ensuring they are relevant and respectful.

- Engaging Communities: Engaging community members in the design and implementation of restorative justice programs to enhance cultural sensitivity and acceptance.

Strategies for Promoting Social Equity Through Restorative Practices

1. Inclusive and Participatory Processes

- Community Engagement: Involving community members in the design, implementation, and evaluation of restorative justice programs to ensure they reflect the diverse needs and perspectives of the community.

- Participant-Centered Approach: Adopting a participant-centered approach that prioritizes the voices and experiences of those affected by harm, promoting inclusivity and empowerment.

2. Training and Capacity Building

- Equity Training: Providing training for restorative justice practitioners on social equity principles and practices, including recognizing and addressing bias and inequality.

- Building Capacity: Investing in capacity building for community members and organizations to enhance their ability to support and participate in restorative justice processes.

3. Policy Advocacy and Reform

- Advocating for Equity: Advocating for policies and reforms that promote social equity within the justice system and broader society, including measures to address systemic inequalities and ensure fair treatment for all.

- Integrating Equity Goals: Integrating social equity goals into restorative justice policies and programs, ensuring they are aligned with broader efforts to promote fairness and justice.

4. Monitoring and Evaluation

- Assessing Impact: Implementing mechanisms for monitoring and evaluating the impact of restorative justice programs on social equity, including collecting and analyzing data on participant demographics, outcomes, and experiences.

- Continuous Improvement: Using evaluation findings to inform continuous improvement and ensure that restorative justice programs are effectively promoting social equity.

Case Studies of Restorative Practices Promoting Social Equity

1. Oakland Unified School District, California

- Background: Oakland Unified School District implemented restorative justice practices to address disparities in school discipline, particularly the disproportionate impact on students of color.

- Restorative Approaches: The district introduced restorative circles, peer mediation, and community-building activities to create a positive school climate and address conflicts constructively.

- Outcomes: The implementation of restorative practices led to a significant reduction in suspensions and expulsions, particularly among students of color, and improved overall school climate and student relationships.

2. Transforming Justice Initiative, New York City

- Background: The Transforming Justice Initiative in New York City focuses on promoting social equity through restorative justice practices within the criminal justice system.

- Restorative Approaches: The initiative offers restorative justice programs for youth and adults, including victim-offender dialogues, community conferencing, and reentry support.

- Outcomes: The initiative has successfully reduced recidivism rates, improved outcomes for marginalized populations, and strengthened community ties by addressing the root causes of harm and promoting healing and accountability.

3. Family Group Conferencing in New Zealand

- Background: New Zealand's Family Group Conferencing (FGC) system was developed to address the overrepresentation of Maori youth in the juvenile justice system and promote culturally relevant restorative practices.

- Restorative Approaches: FGC involves the youth, their family, victims, and community members in a collaborative decision-making process to address harm and develop a plan for reparation and support.

- Outcomes: FGC has successfully reduced reoffending rates among Maori youth, empowered families and communities, and promoted social equity by addressing the specific needs and cultural contexts of participants.

4. Community Holistic Circle Healing (CHCH) in Hollow Water First Nation, Canada

- Background: CHCH was developed in Hollow Water First Nation to address the high rates of sexual abuse and violence within the community using restorative justice principles.

- Restorative Approaches: CHCH involves community members in healing circles, victim-offender dialogues, and community-based support to address harm, promote healing, and restore relationships.

- Outcomes: CHCH has significantly reduced rates of reoffending, promoted healing for victims and offenders, and strengthened community resilience and social equity by addressing the root causes of harm and promoting collective healing.

Conclusion

Restorative justice offers a powerful framework for promoting social equity by addressing harm, fostering accountability, and emphasizing the restoration of relationships and communities. By incorporating principles of fairness, inclusion, and participation, restorative practices can effectively address the unique needs and challenges faced by marginalized and disadvantaged groups. Real-world examples demonstrate the potential of restorative justice to advance social equity and create more just and inclusive societies. The following chapters will continue to explore the transformative potential of restorative justice and its impact on creating a more equitable and compassionate world.

Community Empowerment: Building Stronger, More Resilient Communities

Community empowerment is a fundamental goal of restorative justice, aiming to build stronger, more resilient communities by fostering participation, collaboration, and mutual support. Empowered communities are better equipped to address conflicts, support victims, rehabilitate offenders, and prevent future harm. This chapter explores the principles of community empowerment, the role of restorative justice in fostering empowerment, and strategies for building resilient communities through restorative practices.

Understanding Community Empowerment

1. Definition and Importance

- Community Empowerment: Community empowerment refers to the process of enabling individuals and groups to gain control over their lives, make informed decisions, and actively participate in the development and governance of their communities.

- Importance: Empowered communities are more resilient, cohesive, and capable of addressing challenges and opportunities collectively. Empowerment fosters a sense of ownership, responsibility, and agency among community members.

2. Principles of Community Empowerment

- Participation and Inclusion: Ensuring that all community members have opportunities to participate in decision-making processes and activities that affect their lives.

- Capacity Building: Developing the skills, knowledge, and resources of community members to enable them to take effective action and make informed decisions.

- Collaboration and Partnership: Encouraging collaboration and partnerships among community members, organizations, and institutions to address common goals and challenges.

- Accountability and Transparency: Promoting accountability and transparency in community governance and decision-making processes.

The Role of Restorative Justice in Community Empowerment

1. Fostering Participation and Inclusion

- Inclusive Processes: Restorative justice practices, such as circles and conferencing, create inclusive spaces where all voices are heard and respected. These processes encourage active participation and empower individuals to contribute to conflict resolution and community building.

- Engaging Marginalized Groups: Restorative justice actively seeks to engage marginalized and disadvantaged groups, ensuring that their perspectives and needs are considered in community decision-making.

2. Building Capacity and Skills

- Skill Development: Participation in restorative justice processes helps community members develop essential skills, such as communication, empathy, conflict resolution, and problem-solving.

- Leadership Training: Restorative justice programs often include leadership training and capacity-building initiatives, enabling community members to take on leadership roles and drive positive change.

3. Promoting Collaboration and Partnership

- Community Cohesion: Restorative practices foster collaboration and partnership by bringing together diverse community members to address conflicts and work towards common goals.

- Strengthening Networks: By involving various stakeholders, including schools, local organizations, and justice agencies, restorative justice strengthens community networks and promotes collective action.

4. Enhancing Accountability and Transparency

- Shared Responsibility: Restorative justice emphasizes shared responsibility for addressing harm and promoting healing. This approach encourages accountability among community members and institutions.

- Transparent Processes: Restorative justice processes are transparent, with open communication and clear guidelines, ensuring that all participants understand and trust the process.

Strategies for Building Resilient Communities Through Restorative Practices

1. Implementing Community-Based Restorative Programs

- Local Initiatives: Developing and supporting local restorative justice initiatives that address specific community needs and contexts.

- Sustainable Models: Ensuring that restorative programs are sustainable by securing funding, training facilitators, and building local capacity.

2. Engaging Community Members

- Inclusive Outreach: Conducting inclusive outreach to engage a broad cross-section of the community, including marginalized and underrepresented groups.

- Facilitating Dialogue: Creating opportunities for open dialogue and discussion on community issues, allowing members to voice their concerns and ideas.

3. Building Partnerships and Networks

- Collaborative Approaches: Encouraging collaboration between community organizations, schools, local government, and justice agencies to create a coordinated approach to restorative justice.

- Resource Sharing: Promoting the sharing of resources, knowledge, and expertise among community partners to enhance the effectiveness of restorative initiatives.

4. Providing Training and Capacity Building

- Skill Development Programs: Offering training programs to develop the skills and knowledge of community members, practitioners, and leaders in restorative justice.

- Leadership Development: Supporting leadership development initiatives to empower individuals to take active roles in promoting and sustaining restorative justice in their communities.

5. Monitoring and Evaluating Impact

- Assessing Outcomes: Implementing mechanisms for monitoring and evaluating the impact of restorative justice programs on community empowerment and resilience.

- Continuous Improvement: Using evaluation findings to inform continuous improvement and ensure that programs effectively meet the needs of the community.

Case Studies of Community Empowerment Through Restorative Practices

1. The Hollow Water Community Holistic Circle Healing (CHCH) in Canada

- Background: The CHCH program in Hollow Water First Nation was developed to address high rates of sexual abuse and violence within the community using restorative justice principles.

- Restorative Approaches: The program involves community members in healing circles, victim-offender dialogues, and community-based support to address harm, promote healing, and restore relationships.

- Outcomes: CHCH has significantly reduced rates of reoffending, promoted healing for victims and offenders, and strengthened community resilience and social equity by addressing the root causes of harm and promoting collective healing.

2. Restorative Community Conferencing (RCC) in Oakland, California

- Background: RCC in Oakland focuses on addressing youth offenses through restorative justice practices, involving victims, offenders, and community members in the resolution process.

- Restorative Approaches: RCC facilitates restorative conferences that emphasize accountability, reparation, and community involvement.

- Outcomes: RCC has reduced recidivism rates, improved outcomes for youth of color, and strengthened community ties by addressing the root causes of harm and promoting healing and accountability.

3. Neighborhood Restorative Justice Project (NRJP) in New York City

- Background: The NRJP was established to address low-level offenses and conflicts in neighborhoods through restorative justice practices.

- Restorative Approaches: The project involves community members in restorative circles and mediations to address conflicts, promote reparation, and strengthen community bonds.

- Outcomes: NRJP has successfully resolved numerous conflicts, reduced reliance on the formal justice system, and empowered community members to take an active role in maintaining peace and harmony.

4. Restorative Practices in the U.K.'s Education Sector

- Background: Many schools in the U.K. have adopted restorative practices to address conflicts, reduce bullying, and create positive school climates.

- Restorative Approaches: Schools implement restorative circles, peer mediation, and community-building activities to foster a sense of belonging and mutual respect among students and staff.

- Outcomes: The implementation of restorative practices in schools has led to reduced disciplinary issues, improved student relationships, and enhanced school environments.

Challenges and Considerations

1. Ensuring Sustainability

- Securing Resources: Ensuring the sustainability of restorative justice programs requires securing adequate funding and resources.

- Building Local Capacity: Developing local capacity and leadership is essential for sustaining restorative initiatives over the long term.

2. Addressing Power Imbalances

- Equitable Participation: Addressing power imbalances between participants, such as those based on race, gender, or socioeconomic status, is essential for ensuring fairness and effectiveness in restorative processes.

- Providing Support: Offering support services, such as advocacy and counseling, can help mitigate power imbalances and empower participants.

3. Cultural Sensitivity and Relevance

- Adapting Practices: Adapting restorative practices to fit the cultural contexts and needs of diverse communities is essential for their relevance and effectiveness.

- Engaging Communities: Engaging community members in the design and implementation of restorative justice programs enhances their cultural sensitivity and acceptance.

Conclusion

Community empowerment is a central goal of restorative justice, aiming to build stronger, more resilient communities through participation, collaboration, and mutual support. By fostering inclusive and participatory processes, developing skills and capacity, promoting collaboration, and enhancing accountability and transparency, restorative justice can effectively empower communities to address harm, promote healing, and build a foundation for sustainable peace. Real-world examples demonstrate the transformative potential of restorative justice in fostering community empowerment and resilience, highlighting the importance of these practices in creating more just and compassionate societies. The following chapters will continue to explore the impact of restorative justice on creating a more equitable and compassionate world.

CHAPTER 10

THE FUTURE OF RESTORATIVE JUSTICE

Innovations and Trends: Emerging Trends and Innovations in Restorative Justice

The field of restorative justice is continually evolving, driven by new insights, technological advancements, and changing societal needs. This chapter explores the emerging trends and innovations in restorative justice, highlighting how these developments are shaping the future of the field. From digital restorative practices to integrating restorative justice into new sectors, these innovations promise to enhance the effectiveness, accessibility, and impact of restorative justice worldwide.

Digital and Online Restorative Practices

1. Virtual Mediation and Conferencing

- Background: The rise of digital technology has facilitated the development of virtual mediation and conferencing platforms, enabling restorative justice processes to take place online.

- Advantages: Virtual platforms increase accessibility, allowing participants from different locations to engage in restorative processes without the need for physical presence. They also provide flexibility in scheduling and can reduce logistical barriers.

- Challenges: Ensuring confidentiality, building rapport, and managing emotional intensity can be more challenging in virtual settings. Adequate training for facilitators and robust technological infrastructure are essential.

2. Online Training and Resources

- Background: The availability of online training programs and resources has expanded access to restorative justice education and capacity building.

- Advantages: Online training allows for flexible learning opportunities and can reach a broader audience, including those in remote or underserved areas. It also facilitates continuous professional development for practitioners.

- Challenges: Maintaining engagement and ensuring the quality of online training can be challenging. Combining online learning with in-person training and practical experience can enhance effectiveness.

Integrating Restorative Justice into New Sectors

1. Restorative Practices in Healthcare

- Background: Restorative justice principles are increasingly being applied in the healthcare sector to address conflicts, medical errors, and patient grievances.

- Applications: Restorative practices can be used to facilitate dialogues between patients, families, and healthcare providers, promoting healing, accountability, and trust.

- Benefits: These practices can improve patient satisfaction, reduce litigation, and enhance the overall quality of care.

2. Restorative Practices in Corporate Settings

- Background: Businesses and corporations are adopting restorative justice principles to address workplace conflicts, enhance employee relations, and improve organizational culture.

- Applications: Restorative practices in corporate settings include conflict resolution circles, mediation, and team-building activities focused on open communication and mutual respect.

- Benefits: These practices can reduce workplace conflicts, improve employee morale and productivity, and create a more inclusive and supportive work environment.

3. Restorative Practices in Environmental Justice

- Background: Restorative justice is being explored as a framework for addressing environmental harm and promoting sustainability.

- Applications: Restorative practices can facilitate dialogues between stakeholders affected by environmental issues, promote accountability for environmental harm, and support collaborative efforts to restore ecosystems.

- Benefits: These practices foster a holistic approach to environmental justice, emphasizing the interconnectedness of social, economic, and ecological well-being.

Expanding Restorative Justice in the Criminal Justice System

1. Restorative Justice for Serious Crimes

- Background: While traditionally used for minor offenses, restorative justice is increasingly being applied to serious crimes, including violent offenses and sexual assault.

- Approach: Restorative processes for serious crimes involve careful planning, support for all participants, and a focus on safety and voluntary participation.

- Benefits: These practices can provide meaningful accountability, support victim healing, and promote offender rehabilitation and reintegration.

2. Restorative Justice in Prisons

- Background: Restorative justice programs are being introduced in prisons to address conflicts, support rehabilitation, and prepare inmates for reintegration into society.

- Applications: Programs include restorative circles, victim-offender dialogues, and community service projects.

- Benefits: These practices can reduce recidivism, improve prison culture, and enhance the prospects for successful reintegration.

Innovations in Restorative Justice Research and Evaluation

1. Data-Driven Approaches

- Background: The use of data analytics and evidence-based research is enhancing the evaluation and effectiveness of restorative justice programs.

- Applications: Collecting and analyzing data on program outcomes, participant experiences, and long-term impacts helps refine practices and demonstrate their benefits.

- Benefits: Data-driven approaches support continuous improvement, inform policy decisions, and build credibility and support for restorative justice initiatives.

2. Participatory Action Research

- Background: Participatory action research (PAR) involves engaging community members and participants in the research process to ensure that it reflects their needs and perspectives.

- Applications: PAR can be used to co-design and evaluate restorative justice programs, ensuring that they are responsive to community contexts and priorities.

- Benefits: This approach fosters community ownership, enhances the relevance and impact of research, and empowers participants.

Global Trends and Cross-Cultural Adaptations

1. Cultural Adaptations of Restorative Practices

- Background: Restorative justice is being adapted to fit diverse cultural contexts, ensuring that practices are relevant and respectful of local traditions and values.

- Approach: Collaborating with cultural leaders, incorporating traditional conflict resolution methods, and tailoring practices to local needs.

- Benefits: Cultural adaptations enhance the acceptance and effectiveness of restorative justice, promoting more meaningful and sustainable outcomes.

2. International Collaboration and Knowledge Sharing

- Background: Increased international collaboration and knowledge sharing are fostering the global growth of restorative justice.

- Applications: Conferences, networks, and online platforms facilitate the exchange of best practices, research findings, and innovative approaches.

- Benefits: Global collaboration enhances the development and dissemination of restorative justice, supporting its implementation in diverse contexts.

Case Studies of Innovations and Trends

1. Restorative Justice in the Digital Age: Victim-Offender Dialogue Platforms

- Background: Online platforms for victim-offender dialogues have been developed to facilitate restorative justice processes in a secure and accessible manner.

- Innovations: These platforms use secure video conferencing, digital confidentiality agreements, and online support resources to conduct dialogues.

- Outcomes: Increased accessibility for participants in different locations, reduced logistical barriers, and continued support for restorative justice during the COVID-19 pandemic.

2. Restorative Practices in Corporate Diversity and Inclusion Programs

- Background: Companies are integrating restorative justice principles into their diversity and inclusion programs to address workplace discrimination and promote equity.

- Innovations: Restorative circles and mediation sessions are used to address incidents of discrimination, facilitate open dialogues on diversity, and develop inclusive policies.

- Outcomes: Improved workplace culture, enhanced employee trust and engagement, and progress toward diversity and inclusion goals.

3. Restorative Environmental Justice in New Zealand

- Background: New Zealand is exploring restorative justice approaches to address environmental harm and promote sustainable practices.

- Innovations: Restorative circles involving affected communities, environmental organizations, and policymakers are used to discuss environmental issues, develop restorative actions, and foster collaboration.

- Outcomes: Strengthened community involvement in environmental decision-making, increased accountability for environmental harm, and progress toward sustainability goals.

Conclusion

The future of restorative justice is shaped by emerging trends and innovations that enhance its effectiveness, accessibility, and impact. Digital and online practices, integration into new sectors, expansion within the criminal justice system, and data-driven approaches are driving the evolution of restorative justice. By embracing these innovations and fostering global collaboration, restorative justice can continue to promote healing, accountability, and social equity in diverse contexts. The following chapters will continue to explore the transformative potential of restorative justice and its impact on creating a more just and compassionate world.

Sustainability and Scalability: Ensuring the Long-Term Success and Expansion of Restorative Practices

Ensuring the sustainability and scalability of restorative justice practices is crucial for their long-term success and broader impact. This chapter explores the key factors that contribute to the sustainability of restorative justice programs, strategies for scaling these practices, and case studies that illustrate successful implementation. By focusing on sustainability and scalability, we can ensure that restorative justice continues to evolve and make a meaningful difference in communities worldwide.

Understanding Sustainability and Scalability

1. Sustainability

- Definition: Sustainability in restorative justice refers to the ability of programs to maintain their effectiveness, relevance, and impact over time. It involves securing ongoing funding, building local capacity, and ensuring community support.

- Importance: Sustainable programs are resilient, adaptable, and capable of delivering long-term benefits to individuals and communities.

2. Scalability

- Definition: Scalability refers to the ability to expand restorative justice practices to new settings, regions, and populations while maintaining their effectiveness and quality.

- Importance: Scaling restorative justice practices allows more people and communities to benefit from these approaches, promoting wider social change and justice reform.

Key Factors for Sustainability

1. Funding and Resources

- Securing Funding: Sustainable programs require stable and diverse funding sources, including government grants, private donations, and community fundraising.

- Resource Allocation: Ensuring adequate resources for training, facilitation, support services, and evaluation is essential for maintaining program quality.

2. Capacity Building

- Training Practitioners: Ongoing training and professional development for restorative justice practitioners ensure high-quality facilitation and program delivery.

- Building Community Capacity: Empowering community members with the skills and knowledge to support and participate in restorative practices enhances program sustainability.

3. Community Engagement and Support

- Fostering Buy-In: Building strong relationships with community stakeholders, including local organizations, leaders, and residents, fosters buy-in and support for restorative justice.

- Creating Ownership: Encouraging community ownership of restorative justice programs promotes long-term commitment and sustainability.

4. Institutional Integration

- Policy Support: Advocating for policies that support restorative justice and integrating these practices into existing legal and social systems ensure institutional backing and sustainability.

- Cross-Sector Collaboration: Collaborating with various sectors, such as education, healthcare, and criminal justice, enhances the reach and impact of restorative justice programs.

5. Monitoring and Evaluation

- Continuous Assessment: Implementing mechanisms for regular monitoring and evaluation helps assess program effectiveness, identify areas for improvement, and demonstrate impact.

- Data-Driven Decision Making: Using data and evidence to inform decision-making ensures that programs remain relevant and responsive to community needs.

Strategies for Scalability

1. Model Adaptation and Replication

- Adapting Models: Adapting restorative justice models to fit the unique needs and contexts of different communities is essential for successful scaling.

- Replicating Success: Identifying and replicating successful programs in new settings can expand the reach of restorative justice while maintaining quality and impact.

2. Capacity Building for Scaling

- Training Trainers: Developing a cadre of trainers who can train new practitioners and support the expansion of restorative justice programs is crucial for scalability.

- Resource Development: Creating and disseminating training materials, toolkits, and guidelines can support the consistent and effective implementation of restorative practices.

3. Policy and Advocacy

- Promoting Policy Change: Advocating for policy changes that support the expansion of restorative justice can create an enabling environment for scaling.

- Building Alliances: Forming alliances with advocacy groups, policymakers, and other stakeholders can strengthen efforts to scale restorative justice.

4. Cross-Sector Integration

- Integrating Practices: Integrating restorative justice into various sectors, such as education, criminal justice, and healthcare, can enhance its reach and impact.

- Collaborative Approaches: Developing collaborative approaches that involve multiple sectors and stakeholders can support the scaling of restorative justice practices.

5. Innovative Approaches

- Leveraging Technology: Using digital tools and platforms can facilitate the scaling of restorative justice by increasing accessibility and efficiency.

- Creative Funding Models: Exploring innovative funding models, such as social impact bonds and community investment, can support the expansion of restorative justice programs.

Case Studies of Sustainable and Scalable Restorative Practices

1. New Zealand's Family Group Conferencing (FGC)

- Background: FGC was developed to address the overrepresentation of Maori youth in the juvenile justice system and promote culturally relevant restorative practices.

- Sustainability: The program's sustainability is supported by strong policy backing, continuous training, and community involvement.

- Scalability: FGC has been successfully scaled across New Zealand and adapted in other countries, demonstrating the model's adaptability and effectiveness.

2. Oakland Unified School District, California

- Background: Oakland Unified School District implemented restorative justice practices to address disparities in school discipline and create a positive school climate.

- Sustainability: The program's sustainability is ensured through ongoing funding, training for staff, and strong community partnerships.

- Scalability: The success of the program has led to its expansion within the district and replication in other school districts, highlighting the potential for scaling restorative practices in education.

3. Restorative Justice for Oakland Youth (RJOY)

- Background: RJOY focuses on implementing restorative justice practices in schools, juvenile justice systems, and communities to address racial disparities and promote healing.

- Sustainability: RJOY's sustainability is supported by a combination of grants, donations, and community support, as well as a commitment to continuous learning and adaptation.

- Scalability: The organization's model has been replicated in other cities and states, demonstrating the potential for broader application and impact.

4. Community Holistic Circle Healing (CHCH) in Hollow Water First Nation, Canada

- Background: CHCH was developed to address high rates of sexual abuse and violence within the community using restorative justice principles.

- Sustainability: The program's sustainability is ensured through community ownership, continuous training, and strong support from local leaders.

- Scalability: CHCH's model has been adapted and implemented in other Indigenous communities, showcasing the potential for scaling culturally relevant restorative practices.

Challenges and Considerations for Sustainability and Scalability

1. Maintaining Quality and Fidelity

- Ensuring Consistency: Maintaining the quality and fidelity of restorative practices as they scale is crucial to their effectiveness and impact.

- Training and Support: Providing ongoing training and support for practitioners and facilitators helps ensure consistent and high-quality implementation.

2. Navigating Resistance and Barriers

- Overcoming Resistance: Addressing resistance from stakeholders and institutions that are accustomed to traditional justice approaches is essential for successful scaling.

- Addressing Barriers: Identifying and addressing barriers to participation, such as cost, accessibility, and cultural relevance, is crucial for scaling restorative justice.

3. Balancing Flexibility and Standardization

- Adapting to Contexts: Balancing the need for flexibility to adapt to local contexts with the need for standardization to ensure quality and consistency is a key challenge in scaling.

- Developing Guidelines: Creating adaptable guidelines and frameworks can help maintain consistency while allowing for necessary adaptations.

Conclusion

Ensuring the sustainability and scalability of restorative justice practices is essential for their long-term success and broader impact. By focusing on key factors such as funding, capacity building, community engagement, institutional integration, and continuous evaluation, restorative justice programs can achieve sustainability and expand to new settings and populations. Real-world examples demonstrate the potential for sustainable and scalable restorative practices to promote healing, accountability, and social equity. The following chapters will continue to explore the transformative potential of restorative justice and its impact on creating a more just and compassionate world.

Vision for the Future: A Visionary Look at the Potential of Restorative Justice to Transform Society

Restorative justice holds immense potential to transform society by fostering healing, accountability, and community cohesion. As we look to the future, envisioning a world where restorative practices are integrated into the fabric of our communities and institutions offers hope for a more just, compassionate, and resilient society. This chapter explores the visionary potential of restorative justice, highlighting its transformative impact across various sectors and its role in addressing global challenges.

Envisioning a Restorative Society

1. Core Principles of a Restorative Society

- Healing and Reparation: Prioritizing healing and reparation for victims, offenders, and communities, rather than focusing solely on punishment.

- Accountability and Responsibility: Encouraging individuals and institutions to take responsibility for their actions and their impact on others.

- Inclusivity and Participation: Ensuring that all voices are heard and respected, and that everyone has the opportunity to participate in decision-making processes.

- Community and Relationship Building: Fostering strong, supportive, and interconnected communities that work collaboratively to address conflicts and challenges.

Transforming the Criminal Justice System

1. Restorative Justice as the Norm

- Integration into Legal Frameworks: Envisioning a future where restorative justice is fully integrated into legal frameworks, with restorative practices being the default approach to addressing crime and harm.

- Victim-Centered Approaches: Shifting the focus to prioritize the needs and rights of victims, ensuring they have a central role in the justice process and receive the support they need to heal.

2. Rehabilitation and Reintegration

- Supporting Offender Rehabilitation: Emphasizing rehabilitation and reintegration over punishment, providing offenders with the tools and support needed to make amends and reintegrate into society.

- Reducing Recidivism: Utilizing restorative practices to address the root causes of criminal behavior, reducing recidivism rates, and promoting long-term public safety.

Transforming Education

1. Restorative Schools

- Positive School Climate: Envisioning schools where restorative practices are embedded in the culture, creating a positive, inclusive, and supportive environment for students and staff.

- Addressing Conflicts Constructively: Using restorative circles, mediation, and peer support to address conflicts constructively, reduce bullying, and promote healthy relationships.

2. Empowering Students

- Student Leadership: Empowering students to take active roles in creating a restorative school climate, developing leadership skills, and fostering a sense of ownership and responsibility.

- Social and Emotional Learning: Integrating restorative practices with social and emotional learning curricula to help students develop empathy, communication skills, and emotional resilience.

Transforming Communities

1. Community Cohesion and Resilience

- Building Strong Communities: Envisioning communities where restorative practices are used to build strong, cohesive, and resilient networks of support, fostering mutual aid and collective problem-solving.

- Addressing Local Conflicts: Utilizing community-based restorative practices to address local conflicts, reduce violence, and promote social harmony.

2. Inclusive Decision-Making

- Participatory Governance: Promoting participatory governance models where community members are actively involved in decision-making processes, ensuring that policies and initiatives reflect the needs and values of the community.

- Collaborative Solutions: Encouraging collaborative approaches to addressing social issues, leveraging the strengths and resources of diverse community members.

Addressing Global Challenges

1. Restorative Environmental Justice

- Healing the Planet: Applying restorative justice principles to address environmental harm, promoting accountability for environmental degradation, and fostering collaborative efforts to restore ecosystems.

- Community Involvement: Engaging communities in environmental decision-making processes, ensuring that those most affected by environmental issues have a voice and role in creating solutions.

2. Global Peacebuilding

Post-Conflict Reconciliation: Utilizing restorative justice in post-conflict settings to promote healing, reconciliation, and sustainable peace, addressing the root causes of conflict and supporting long-term recovery.

- Cross-Cultural Dialogue: Fostering cross-cultural dialogue and understanding through restorative practices, promoting global solidarity and cooperation.

Embracing Innovation and Technology

1. Digital Restorative Practices

- Expanding Access: Leveraging technology to expand access to restorative justice, enabling virtual mediation, conferencing, and support services that can reach diverse and remote populations.

- Enhancing Communication: Using digital tools to enhance communication, documentation, and evaluation of restorative practices, ensuring transparency and accountability.

2. Innovative Approaches

- Creative Solutions: Encouraging innovative approaches to restorative justice, such as integrating restorative practices with art, storytelling, and other creative modalities to promote healing and expression.

- Research and Development: Investing in research and development to continuously improve and adapt restorative practices, ensuring they remain relevant and effective in addressing emerging challenges.

Fostering a Culture of Restorative Justice

1. Public Awareness and Education

- Raising Awareness: Promoting public awareness of restorative justice principles and practices through education campaigns, media, and community outreach.

- Educational Curricula: Integrating restorative justice education into school curricula, professional training programs, and higher education to build a foundational understanding of restorative principles.

2. Cultivating Restorative Values

- Values-Based Culture: Fostering a culture that embraces restorative values, such as empathy, compassion, accountability, and respect, in all aspects of society.

- Role Models and Champions: Encouraging leaders, influencers, and role models to champion restorative justice and exemplify restorative values in their actions and decisions.

Conclusion

The vision for the future of restorative justice is one of profound transformation, where restorative practices are deeply embedded in the fabric of society, promoting healing, accountability, and community cohesion. By integrating restorative justice into the criminal justice system, education, communities, and global efforts, we can create a more just, compassionate, and resilient world. Embracing innovation and technology, fostering public awareness, and cultivating restorative values are essential steps toward realizing this vision. The transformative potential of restorative justice offers hope for a brighter future, where individuals and communities can thrive in harmony and justice.

CONCLUSION

Conclusion: Summary of Key Points

Recap of Main Themes and Insights

This book has explored the multifaceted dimensions of restorative justice, emphasizing its transformative potential in promoting healing, accountability, and community cohesion. The journey through the various chapters has provided a comprehensive understanding of restorative justice principles, practices, and their impact on individuals, communities, and society at large. This concluding chapter summarizes the key points and themes discussed, highlighting the central insights and takeaways.

Historical Foundations and Theoretical Frameworks

1. Ancient Practices and Historical Roots

   - Restorative justice is rooted in ancient practices and cultural traditions that emphasize community involvement, reparation, and healing.

- Historical examples from Indigenous cultures and early societies demonstrate the longstanding value of restorative approaches in maintaining social harmony.

2. Philosophical Underpinnings

- The theoretical foundations of restorative justice are built on key philosophical theories that prioritize human dignity, empathy, and interconnectedness.

- Ethical considerations in restorative justice focus on morality, the philosophy of punishment, and the balance between individual and collective justice.

Core Principles and Values

1. Accountability and Responsibility

- Restorative justice emphasizes the importance of taking responsibility for one's actions and making amends to those harmed.

- Accountability is a cornerstone of restorative practices, fostering personal growth and behavioral change.

2. Reparation and Healing

- Reparation involves making amends for harm caused, addressing both material and emotional needs of victims.

- Healing is a central goal, promoting emotional recovery and reconciliation for all parties involved.

3. Community Involvement and Empathy

- Community involvement is crucial for the success of restorative justice, providing support and fostering collective responsibility.

- Empathy and emotional healing are fostered through restorative practices, encouraging understanding and connection between victims, offenders, and the community.

Restorative Practices and Models

1. Victim-Offender Mediation and Family Group Conferencing

- Victim-offender mediation provides a platform for direct dialogue, promoting mutual understanding and agreement on reparative actions.

- Family group conferencing involves family and community in resolving conflicts, emphasizing collaborative decision-making and support.

2. Circle Processes and Community Restorative Boards

- Circle processes facilitate open and inclusive discussions, promoting healing and resolution through collective dialogue.

- Community restorative boards engage community members in addressing offenses and supporting offender reintegration.

Case Studies and Real-world Applications

1. Criminal Justice System

- Restorative justice has been effectively integrated into various criminal justice systems, addressing both minor and serious offenses.

- Examples from New Zealand, Canada, and South Africa illustrate the positive impact of restorative justice on reducing recidivism and promoting victim satisfaction.

2. Schools and Educational Settings

- Restorative practices in schools address bullying, reduce disciplinary issues, and create positive learning environments.

- Programs in the United States and the United Kingdom demonstrate the success of restorative approaches in improving school climate and student relationships.

3. Workplace and Organizations

- Restorative justice is increasingly applied in corporate and organizational settings to address conflicts and enhance employee relations.

- Examples from various sectors highlight the benefits of restorative practices in promoting a supportive and inclusive workplace culture.

4. Community Programs

- Community-based restorative justice programs address local conflicts, strengthen social bonds, and promote collective healing.

- Initiatives in Canada, the United States, and Brazil demonstrate the effectiveness of community-driven restorative practices.

Benefits and Challenges

1. Positive Outcomes

- Restorative justice offers numerous benefits, including victim empowerment, offender rehabilitation, and community cohesion.

- Evidence shows that restorative practices reduce recidivism, improve victim satisfaction, and enhance social harmony.

2. Common Challenges

- Implementing restorative justice faces challenges such as resistance to change, resource constraints, and ensuring voluntary participation.

- Addressing power imbalances and creating safe, inclusive environments are crucial for the success of restorative practices.

3. Criticisms and Controversies

- Critics argue that restorative justice can be perceived as lenient and may lead to inconsistent outcomes.

- Ensuring fairness, voluntary participation, and addressing systemic biases are essential to overcoming these criticisms.

Future Directions and Innovations

1. Emerging Trends and Innovations

- Digital restorative practices and online platforms expand access and flexibility, facilitating virtual mediation and conferencing.

- Integrating restorative justice into new sectors, such as healthcare and environmental justice, demonstrates its adaptability and broad potential.

2. Sustainability and Scalability

- Ensuring the sustainability of restorative programs requires stable funding, capacity building, and community support.

- Strategies for scaling include adapting models, building partnerships, and leveraging technology to reach wider populations.

3. Vision for the Future

- Envisioning a restorative society involves integrating restorative practices into all aspects of life, promoting healing, accountability, and social equity.

- Restorative justice has the potential to transform criminal justice, education, communities, and global peacebuilding efforts, creating a more just and compassionate world.

Conclusion

Restorative justice offers a powerful and transformative approach to addressing harm, promoting healing, and fostering community cohesion. By embracing restorative principles and practices, we can create more just and equitable societies where individuals are supported, relationships are restored, and communities thrive. The insights and examples presented in this book highlight the profound impact of restorative justice and its potential to shape a brighter future for all.

Conclusion: Call to Action

Encouragement for Readers to Engage with and Support Restorative Justice Initiatives

The journey through this book has illuminated the profound potential of restorative justice to transform lives, communities, and societies. As we conclude, it is essential to move from understanding and appreciation to action. This chapter serves as a call to action, encouraging readers to engage with and support restorative justice initiatives in their communities and beyond. By taking active steps, each of us can contribute to creating a more just, compassionate, and resilient world.

Understanding Your Role in Restorative Justice

1. Individual Engagement

- Educate Yourself and Others: Continuously seek to learn more about restorative justice principles and practices. Share your knowledge with friends, family, and colleagues to raise awareness.

- Participate in Restorative Processes: If you are directly affected by conflict or harm, consider participating in restorative justice processes to experience its benefits firsthand.

- Volunteer: Offer your time and skills to local restorative justice programs. Many organizations need volunteers to assist with facilitation, outreach, and support services.

2. Community Involvement

- Support Local Initiatives: Identify and support restorative justice programs and initiatives in your community. Attend events, contribute financially, and advocate for their work.

- Promote Restorative Practices: Encourage schools, workplaces, and community organizations to adopt restorative practices. Share success stories and evidence of their impact.

- Engage with Policy Makers: Advocate for policies that integrate restorative justice into the criminal justice system, education, and other sectors. Write to your representatives, join advocacy groups, and participate in public discussions.

Practical Steps to Support Restorative Justice

1. Advocacy and Awareness

- Raise Public Awareness: Use social media, blogs, and public speaking opportunities to highlight the benefits of restorative justice. Share articles, videos, and personal stories to engage a broader audience.

- Organize Community Events: Host workshops, seminars, and discussion groups to educate your community about restorative justice and its applications.

- Collaborate with Media: Work with local media to cover restorative justice stories, highlight program successes, and promote public understanding.

2. Building Restorative Justice Networks

- Connect with Practitioners: Join restorative justice networks and organizations to connect with practitioners, share resources, and collaborate on projects.

- Establish Partnerships: Build partnerships with schools, businesses, faith communities, and other organizations to promote and implement restorative practices.

- Foster Peer Support: Create or join peer support groups for individuals involved in restorative justice, providing a platform for sharing experiences and mutual encouragement.

3. Funding and Resources

- Fundraising Efforts: Organize fundraising events, campaigns, and initiatives to support restorative justice programs. Engage your network to contribute financially or in-kind.

- Grant Writing: Assist local programs in applying for grants and other funding opportunities. Share information about available grants and provide support in the application process.

- Resource Sharing: Donate materials, space, and other resources to restorative justice programs. Offer professional services such as training, legal advice, or counseling.

Personal Development and Commitment

1. Reflect on Your Values

- Align with Restorative Principles: Reflect on how restorative justice principles align with your personal values and beliefs. Commit to integrating these principles into your daily life and interactions.

- Cultivate Empathy: Practice empathy and active listening in your relationships. Seek to understand and address the needs and perspectives of others.

2. Continuous Learning

- Pursue Further Education: Enroll in courses, workshops, and training programs to deepen your understanding of restorative justice. Stay updated on the latest research and developments in the field.

- Learn from Experience: Reflect on your experiences with restorative justice, whether as a participant, volunteer or advocate. Use these reflections to improve your practice and advocacy.

3. Mentorship and Leadership

- Mentor Others: Share your knowledge and experience with others who are new to restorative justice. Offer guidance and support to those interested in becoming practitioners or advocates.

- Lead by Example: Demonstrate restorative justice principles in your leadership roles. Foster inclusive, participatory, and compassionate environments in your community and workplace.

Inspiring Stories and Examples

1. Community Transformation

- Oakland Unified School District: The adoption of restorative justice practices in Oakland schools has significantly reduced suspensions and expulsions, creating a more positive and inclusive school climate.

- Restorative Community Conferencing in New Zealand: The success of Family Group Conferencing in New Zealand has demonstrated the potential of restorative justice to address youth offenses and support community healing.

2. Individual Impact

- Restorative Circles in Prisons: Programs like those in the Green Bay Correctional Institution in Wisconsin have shown how restorative circles can transform the lives of inmates, promoting accountability, empathy, and rehabilitation.

- Victim-Offender Mediation Success Stories: Numerous cases of victim-offender mediation have resulted in profound healing and reconciliation, demonstrating the power of dialogue and reparation.

Vision for the Future

1. A Restorative World

- Global Adoption: Imagine a world where restorative justice is the norm in addressing conflict and harm.

Visualize schools, workplaces, and communities that embrace restorative principles in all interactions.

- Sustainable Peace: Envision a future where restorative justice contributes to sustainable peace and justice globally, addressing the root causes of conflict and promoting healing and reconciliation.

2. Collective Responsibility

- Shared Vision: Embrace the shared vision of a restorative society. Recognize that each of us has a role to play in making this vision a reality.

- Active Engagement: Commit to active engagement with restorative justice initiatives, understanding that collective action is essential for lasting change.

Conclusion

Restorative justice offers a transformative approach to addressing harm, promoting healing, and fostering community cohesion. As we move forward, each of us has the power to contribute to the growth and success of restorative justice initiatives. By engaging with and supporting these practices, we can help build a more just, compassionate, and resilient society. Let this call to action inspire you to take meaningful steps towards embracing and promoting restorative justice in your life and community. Together, we can create a brighter future for all.

Conclusion: Final Thoughts

Reflections on the Transformative Power of Restorative Justice

As we conclude this exploration of restorative justice, it is vital to reflect on its profound transformative power. Restorative justice is more than a set of practices; it is a philosophy and way of being that prioritizes healing, accountability, and community cohesion. The insights gained throughout this book illuminate how restorative justice can reshape our responses to harm, foster stronger relationships, and build more just and compassionate communities.

The Essence of Restorative Justice

1. Healing and Reparation

   - Central to Restorative Justice: At its core, restorative justice is about healing the harm caused by wrongdoing. It seeks to repair the damage done to victims, offenders, and the broader community.

   - Humanizing Approach: By focusing on the needs of all parties involved, restorative justice humanizes the process of addressing harm, emphasizing empathy, understanding, and reparation.

2. Accountability and Responsibility

   - Encouraging Accountability: Restorative justice encourages offenders to take responsibility for their actions, promoting genuine accountability rather than mere punishment.

- Transformative Potential: This accountability fosters personal growth and behavioral change, which can lead to transformative outcomes for offenders and their communities.

3. Community and Relationship Building

- Strengthening Social Bonds: Restorative justice practices strengthen the social fabric by fostering collaboration, mutual support, and collective problem-solving.

- Restoring Trust: By addressing conflicts and harms in a restorative manner, communities can rebuild trust and resilience, paving the way for long-term harmony and cohesion.

The Broader Impact of Restorative Justice

1. Criminal Justice System

- Alternative to Retribution: Restorative justice provides a compelling alternative to the traditional retributive justice system, offering pathways for rehabilitation and reintegration.

- Reducing Recidivism: Evidence shows that restorative practices reduce recidivism rates, contributing to safer communities and more effective justice outcomes.

2. Education and Schools

- Positive School Climate: Implementing restorative practices in schools transforms the educational environment, reducing disciplinary issues and fostering a culture of respect and inclusion.

- Empowering Students: By involving students in restorative processes, schools empower young people to develop conflict resolution skills and take ownership of their actions.

3. Workplace and Organizations

- Enhancing Workplace Culture: Restorative justice can transform workplace dynamics, resolving conflicts constructively and promoting a culture of openness and mutual respect.

- Improving Employee Relations: Organizations that embrace restorative practices often see improved employee relations, higher morale, and increased productivity.

4. Community Building

- Addressing Local Conflicts: Restorative justice helps communities address local conflicts and tensions, promoting social harmony and collective well-being.

- Fostering Inclusivity: By involving diverse community members in restorative processes, these practices promote inclusivity and equity, addressing systemic inequalities and fostering social justice.

Embracing Restorative Justice for a Better Future

1. A Vision for Transformation

- Envisioning Change: Imagine a world where restorative justice principles guide our responses to conflict and harm, where healing and accountability are prioritized over punishment and exclusion.

- Creating Inclusive Communities: Envision communities where every individual feels valued, supported, and empowered to contribute to the collective good.

2. Collective Responsibility

- Shared Commitment: Achieving the vision of a restorative society requires a collective commitment from individuals, communities, and institutions.

- Active Participation: Each of us has a role to play in promoting and supporting restorative justice, whether through advocacy, participation or simply embodying restorative values in our daily lives.

3. Hope for the Future

- Inspiring Change: The transformative power of restorative justice offers hope for a future where justice systems are more humane, communities are more resilient, and individuals are more connected.

- Building a Just World: By embracing restorative justice, we can work towards building a world that is more just, compassionate, and inclusive for future generations.

Final Thoughts

Restorative justice is a powerful tool for transforming our responses to harm and conflict. It challenges us to look beyond punishment and retribution, to focus on healing, accountability, and the restoration of relationships. The journey through this book has highlighted the profound impact of restorative justice in various contexts, demonstrating its potential to create meaningful change in individuals and communities.

As we reflect on the insights and lessons learned, it is clear that restorative justice offers a path towards a more just and compassionate world. It calls on us to embrace empathy, foster collaboration, and take responsibility for creating a society where everyone can thrive. The transformative power of restorative justice lies in its ability to bring people together, to heal wounds, and to build stronger, more resilient communities.

Let us carry forward the principles and practices of restorative justice, championing its values in our personal and professional lives. Together, we can contribute to a brighter future, where justice is restorative, communities are cohesive, and every individual is treated with dignity and respect.

APPENDIX

Glossary of Terms

This glossary provides definitions of key terms and concepts related to restorative justice. It is intended to serve as a reference for readers to better understand the terminology used throughout this book.

A

Accountability: The obligation of offenders to take responsibility for their actions, acknowledge the harm they have caused, and participate in processes to make amends and repair the damage.

Adversarial System: A legal system, such as that in the United States and many other countries, where the prosecution and defense oppose each other in court, and a judge or jury determines the outcome.

Apology: Acknowledgment of wrongdoing by the offender, expressing remorse and willingness to make amends to the victim.

B

Bias: Prejudice in favor of or against a person, group, or idea, often in a way that is considered to be unfair. In restorative justice, addressing biases is crucial for ensuring fair and equitable processes.

Bullying: Repeated aggressive behavior intended to hurt another person physically, mentally, or emotionally. Restorative practices in schools often address bullying through dialogue and reparation.

C

Circle Process: A restorative practice that involves participants sitting in a circle to discuss issues, share perspectives, and make decisions collectively. It emphasizes equality, respect, and open communication.

Community Conferencing: A restorative process where offenders, victims, and community members come together to discuss the harm caused and develop a plan to repair it and prevent future incidents.

Community Restorative Board: A group of community volunteers who meet with offenders to discuss the harm caused by their actions and determine appropriate reparative actions.

Conflict Resolution: The process of resolving a dispute or conflict by providing each side's needs and addressing their interests.

D

Dialogue: A structured conversation between two or more parties, often facilitated, that focuses on sharing experiences, understanding different perspectives, and finding common ground.

Diversion: Redirecting offenders away from the formal justice system and into restorative justice programs or other alternative measures, often to prevent the negative impacts of formal judicial processes.

E

Empathy: The ability to understand and share the feelings of another. Empathy is a key component of restorative justice, helping to foster understanding and healing between victims and offenders.

Equity: Fairness and justice in the way people are treated. In restorative justice, equity involves addressing power imbalances and ensuring that all participants have an equal voice.

F

Family Group Conferencing (FGC): A restorative practice that involves family members and others significant to the offender and victim in developing a plan to address the harm and support rehabilitation.

G

Gacaca Courts: Community-based tribunals in Rwanda used to address crimes related to the 1994 genocide, emphasizing truth-telling, accountability, and community healing.

H

Healing: The process of recovering from harm or trauma. In restorative justice, healing involves addressing emotional, physical, and relational wounds.

Harm: The injury or damage caused by a wrongful act. Restorative justice seeks to address and repair the harm caused to victims, offenders, and communities.

I

Inclusion: Ensuring that all voices are heard and respected in restorative processes. Inclusion is essential for fairness and the legitimacy of restorative justice outcomes.

Interconnectedness: The concept that all individuals and communities are linked and that actions affecting one part of the community can impact the whole.

M

Mediation: A facilitated process in which a neutral third party helps disputants communicate and negotiate to reach a mutually agreeable resolution.

O

Offender: A person who has committed a wrongful act or crime. In restorative justice, offenders are encouraged to take responsibility for their actions and make amends.

P

Participation: The active involvement of all affected parties in restorative justice processes. Participation ensures that everyone has a voice and contributes to the resolution.

Peacemaking Circles: A type of circle process focused on resolving conflicts and promoting healing and reconciliation within communities.

R

Reconciliation: The process of restoring relationships and resolving conflicts, often involving forgiveness and mutual understanding between victims and offenders.

Reparation: Actions taken by offenders to repair the harm they have caused, which may include apologies, restitution, community service, or other forms of making amends.

Restorative Justice: An approach to justice that focuses on repairing harm, involving all affected parties, and addressing the needs of victims, offenders, and the community.

Restorative Practices: A range of practices and processes that apply restorative justice principles in various contexts, such as schools, workplaces, and communities.

S

School-to-Prison Pipeline: The policies and practices that push students, particularly those from marginalized communities, out of schools and into the criminal justice system. Restorative justice in schools aims to disrupt this pipeline by addressing conflicts constructively.

Survivor: A person who has experienced harm or victimization. In restorative justice, survivors are central to the process and their needs and perspectives are prioritized.

T

Truth and Reconciliation Commission (TRC): A restorative justice process used in post-conflict or post-authoritarian contexts to address historical injustices, uncover the truth, and promote healing and reconciliation.

Trauma-Informed Approach: An approach that recognizes the impact of trauma on individuals and incorporates this understanding into restorative practices to ensure sensitivity and support for affected parties.

V

Victim: A person who has been harmed by a wrongful act. In restorative justice, victims' needs, rights, and perspectives are central to the process.

Victim-Offender Mediation: A facilitated dialogue between victims and offenders, aimed at addressing the harm caused, promoting understanding, and developing a reparative agreement.

W

Whole-School Approach: Implementing restorative practices throughout a school, involving all staff, students, and policies, to create a restorative school climate.

This glossary serves as a reference to better understand the key terms and concepts used in restorative justice. Familiarity with these terms will enhance your comprehension of the principles and practices discussed throughout this book, supporting your engagement with and advocacy for restorative justice initiatives.

RESOURCES AND FURTHER READING

Recommended Books

1. "The Little Book of Restorative Justice" by Howard Zehr

- A foundational text that provides a comprehensive overview of restorative justice principles and practices. Zehr is often referred to as the "grandfather of restorative justice."

2. "Changing Lenses: A New Focus for Crime and Justice" by Howard Zehr

- This book challenges traditional views of justice and proposes a restorative approach focused on healing and reconciliation.

3. "Restorative Justice: Ideas, Values, Debates" by Gerry Johnstone

- A thorough exploration of the ideas and values underpinning restorative justice, as well as the debates surrounding its implementation.

4. "The Little Book of Circle Processes: A New/Old Approach to Peacemaking" by Kay Pranis

- An introduction to the use of circle processes in restorative justice, with practical guidance on facilitating circles.

5. "Restorative Justice in Schools: A Practical Guide" by Bill Hansberry

- A practical guide for educators and school administrators on implementing restorative justice practices in schools.

6. "The Restorative Justice Pocketbook" by Margaret Thorsborne and David Vinegrad

- A concise and practical resource for understanding and applying restorative practices in various settings.

7. "Peacemaking Circles: From Crime to Community" by Kay Pranis, Barry Stuart, and Mark Wedge

- An exploration of the use of peacemaking circles to address conflicts and build stronger communities.

8. "The Little Book of Restorative Discipline for Schools" by Lorraine Stutzman Amstutz and Judy H. Mullet

- This book focuses on how restorative practices can be used to create a positive school environment and address disciplinary issues.

9. "Restorative Justice and Responsive Regulation" by John Braithwaite

- An examination of how restorative justice principles can be integrated into regulatory systems to create more effective and responsive governance.

10. "Restorative Practices and Bullying: Rethinking Behavior Management" by Margaret Thorsborne and David Vinegrad

- A detailed look at how restorative practices can be used to address bullying and create a more supportive school culture.

RECOMMENDED ARTICLES

1. "Restorative Justice: The Evidence" by Lawrence W. Sherman and Heather Strang

   - An in-depth review of the empirical evidence supporting the effectiveness of restorative justice practices.

2. "Restorative Justice and Youth Justice: Bringing Theory and Practice Closer Together in Europe" by Adam Crawford and Tim Newburn

   - A discussion of the integration of restorative justice into youth justice systems in Europe.

3. "Restorative Justice: The Concept" by Howard Zehr and Ali Gohar

   - An overview of the concept of restorative justice, its principles, and its application in various contexts.

4. "Victim Satisfaction with Restorative Justice: More Than Simply Procedural Justice" by Carolyn Hoyle, Richard Young, and Roderick Hill

- An exploration of the factors contributing to victim satisfaction in restorative justice processes.

5. "The Use of Restorative Justice Practices in a School Community" by Brenda Morrison

- A case study on the implementation of restorative justice practices in a school setting and their impact on school culture and student behavior.

Recommended Organizations

1. Restorative Justice International (RJI)

- A global association dedicated to promoting restorative justice principles and practices. RJI offers resources, training, and advocacy to support the growth of restorative justice worldwide.

- Website: www.restorativejusticeinternational.com

2. International Institute for Restorative Practices (IIRP)

- A graduate school and training institute focused on restorative practices. IIRP provides education, research, and resources to advance restorative practices in various fields.

- Website: www.iirp.edu

3. Centre for Justice & Reconciliation

An organization dedicated to promoting restorative justice through research, advocacy, and program development. The Centre offers a wealth of resources, including publications and training materials.

-   Website: www.restorativejustice.org

4. Restorative Justice Council (RJC)

- A UK-based organization that promotes restorative justice by setting standards, providing accreditation, and offering training and resources for practitioners.

-   Website: www.restorativejustice.org.uk

5. National Association of Community and Restorative Justice (NACRJ)

- A professional organization that supports the development and implementation of restorative and community justice practices in the United States.

- Website: www.nacrj.org

6. Restorative Justice Network of Ireland (RJNI)

- An organization focused on promoting and supporting restorative justice practices throughout Ireland through networking, training, and advocacy.

- Website: www.restorativejustice.ie

7. European Forum for Restorative Justice (EFRJ)

- A network of organizations and individuals dedicated to promoting restorative justice throughout Europe through research, advocacy, and training.

- Website: www.euforumrj.org

8. Centre for Restorative Justice at Simon Fraser University

- A research and education center focused on advancing restorative justice through academic programs, research projects, and community partnerships.

- Website: www.sfu.ca/crj

9. The Little Book of Restorative Justice Series

- A series of accessible books that provide introductions to various aspects of restorative justice, authored by leading practitioners and scholars in the field.

- Publisher: Good Books

Online Resources

1. Restorative Justice Clearinghouse (RJC)

- An online repository of resources, including articles, reports, and toolkits, related to restorative justice.

- Website: www.restorativejustice.org

2. IIRP Graduate School's Online Library

- A comprehensive collection of articles, research papers, and resources on restorative practices, available for free online.

- Website: www.iirp.edu/library

3. TED Talks on Restorative Justice

- A collection of TED Talks by experts and practitioners discussing various aspects of restorative justice and its impact.

- Website: www.ted.com

This appendix provides a starting point for further exploration and engagement with restorative justice. By delving into these resources, readers can deepen their understanding, expand their skills, and become more effective advocates for restorative practices in their communities.

SAMPLE RESTORATIVE PRACTICES

Templates and Guidelines for Implementing Restorative Practices

This appendix provides practical templates and guidelines for implementing restorative practices in various settings, including schools, workplaces, and communities. These resources are designed to help practitioners and stakeholders effectively facilitate restorative processes, promoting healing, accountability, and community cohesion.

1. Restorative Circles

Restorative Circle Process Template

Purpose: To facilitate open dialogue and mutual understanding, address conflicts, and develop collective solutions.

Participants: Facilitator, individuals involved in the conflict, and other relevant community members.

Materials Needed:

- Talking piece (an object passed around to indicate who has the floor)

- Chairs arranged in a circle

- Flip chart or whiteboard (optional)

Steps:

1. Opening the Circle:

- Welcome participants and explain the purpose of the circle.

- Set ground rules (e.g., respect, confidentiality, speaking one at a time).

- Introduce the talking piece and explain its use.

2. Check-In:

- Conduct a check-in round where each participant shares how they are feeling.

- Use an open-ended question to encourage sharing (e.g., "What brings you here today?").

3. Storytelling:

- Invite participants to share their perspectives on the conflict or issue.

- Encourage active listening and empathy.

4. Identifying Needs and Concerns:

- Use a round to identify the needs and concerns of each participant.

- Summarize and clarify these needs to ensure mutual understanding.

5. Generating Solutions:

- Facilitate a brainstorming session to generate potential solutions.

- Encourage collaborative problem-solving and consider all suggestions.

6. Agreement and Action Plan:

- Develop a consensus on the actions needed to address the issue.

- Create a written action plan outlining responsibilities and timelines.

7. Check-Out:

- Conduct a check-out round where participants reflect on the process and share final thoughts.

- Express appreciation for participation and commitment to the agreement.

8. Closing the Circle:

- Formally close the circle and thank participants for their contributions.

2. Victim-Offender Mediation

Victim-Offender Mediation Process Template

Purpose: To facilitate a structured dialogue between the victim and offender, promoting understanding, accountability, and reparation.

Participants: Mediator, victim, offender, and support persons (if applicable).

Materials Needed:

- Private, neutral meeting space

- Notepads and pens

- Agreement form

Steps:

1. Preparation:

   - Meet separately with the victim and offender to explain the process and gather background information.

   - Ensure both parties are willing to participate voluntarily.

2. Introduction:

   - Welcome participants and explain the mediation process and ground rules.

   - Establish confidentiality and the role of the mediator as a neutral facilitator.

3. Victim's Story:

   - Allow the victim to share their experience, the impact of the offense, and their feelings.

- Encourage the offender to listen actively without interruption.

4. Offender's Response:

- Give the offender the opportunity to respond, share their perspective, and express remorse.

- Encourage the victim to listen actively without interruption.

5. Dialogue and Discussion:

- Facilitate an open dialogue between the victim and offender, addressing questions and concerns.

- Guide the conversation to focus on understanding, accountability, and empathy.

6. Reparation and Agreement:

- Discuss possible ways for the offender to make amends and address the victim's needs.

- Develop a written agreement outlining the reparation actions and timelines.

7. Follow-Up Plan:

- Establish a follow-up plan to monitor the implementation of the agreement.

- Schedule additional meetings if necessary to review progress.

8. Conclusion:

- Thank participants for their openness and willingness to engage in the process.

- Provide contact information for ongoing support if needed.

3. Family Group Conferencing (FGC)

Family Group Conferencing Process Template

Purpose: To involve the family and community in addressing conflicts and developing a collective plan to support the offender and victim.

Participants: Facilitator, offender, victim, family members, and community supporters.

Materials Needed:

- Meeting space suitable for a large group

- Flip chart or whiteboard

- Notepads and pens

- Agreement form

Steps:

1. Preparation:

- Meet with the offender, victim, and their families separately to explain the process and gather background information.

- Ensure that all participants understand the purpose and voluntarily agree to participate.

2. Introduction:

- Welcome participants and explain the FGC process and ground rules.

- Introduce all participants and clarify their roles.

3. Sharing Perspectives:

- Invite the victim to share their experience and the impact of the offense.

- Allow the offender to respond and share their perspective.

4. Family and Community Input:

- Encourage family members and community supporters to share their thoughts and feelings.

- Discuss the impact of the offense on the family and community.

5. Private Family Time:

- Allow the family and community supporters private time to discuss and develop a plan to address the harm and support the offender and victim.

- The facilitator remains available for questions but does not participate in the discussion.

6. Developing the Action Plan:

- Reconvene the group and present the family's plan.

- Discuss and refine the plan with input from all participants.

- Ensure that the plan addresses reparation, accountability, and support.

7. Agreement and Commitment:

- Create a written agreement detailing the action plan, responsibilities, and timelines.

- Ensure that all participants commit to the plan and understand their roles.

8. Follow-Up and Review:

- Establish a follow-up schedule to monitor the implementation of the agreement.

- Plan additional meetings if necessary to review progress and make adjustments.

9. Conclusion:

- Thank participants for their contributions and commitment to the process.

- Provide contact information for ongoing support and resources.

4. Restorative Practices in Schools

Restorative Practices in Schools Template

Purpose: To create a positive school climate, address conflicts, and promote student accountability and empathy.

Participants: Students, teachers, administrators, and support staff.

Materials Needed:

- Classroom or meeting space

- Talking piece (for circle processes)

- Flip chart or whiteboard

- Notepads and pens

Steps:

1. Establishing Restorative Culture:

- Train staff and students in restorative practices and principles.

- Integrate restorative practices into school policies and procedures.

2. Restorative Circles:

- Use restorative circles for regular classroom meetings, conflict resolution, and community building.

- Establish ground rules and ensure that all voices are heard and respected.

3. Peer Mediation:

- Train students as peer mediators to help resolve conflicts among their peers.

- Create a referral system for students to seek peer mediation support.

4. Restorative Conferences:

- Conduct restorative conferences for more serious conflicts or incidents.

- Involve the affected parties, their families, and school staff in developing a plan for reparation and support.

5. Proactive Circles:

- Hold proactive circles regularly to build relationships, discuss classroom issues, and create a sense of community.

- Use circles to address topics such as bullying, inclusivity, and empathy.

6. Responsive Circles:

- Use responsive circles to address specific incidents of harm or conflict.

- Focus on understanding the impact, addressing the needs of those affected, and developing a plan for reparation.

7. Restorative Discipline Policies:

- Replace punitive discipline policies with restorative approaches that focus on accountability, reparation, and personal growth.

- Ensure that disciplinary actions are fair, consistent, and restorative in nature.

8. Ongoing Support and Training:

- Provide ongoing support and training for staff and students to maintain and strengthen restorative practices.

- Create a restorative practices committee to oversee implementation and address challenges.

Conclusion

These templates and guidelines provide practical steps for implementing restorative practices in various settings. By following these processes, practitioners can foster healing, accountability, and community cohesion, contributing to a more just and compassionate society. Whether in schools, workplaces, or communities, restorative practices offer a powerful tool for addressing harm and building stronger, more resilient relationships.

REFERENCES

Bibliography

This comprehensive bibliography includes all the references and sources cited throughout the book. These works provide foundational knowledge, empirical evidence, and practical guidance on restorative justice principles and practices.

Books

1. Zehr, H. (2002). The Little Book of Restorative Justice. Good Books.

2. Zehr, H. (2005). Changing Lenses: A New Focus for Crime and Justice. Herald Press.

3. Johnstone, G. (2011). Restorative Justice: Ideas, Values, Debates. Routledge.

4. Pranis, K. (2005). The Little Book of Circle Processes: A New/Old Approach to Peacemaking. Good Books.

5. Hansberry, B. (2016). Restorative Justice in Schools: A Practical Guide. Jessica Kingsley Publishers.

6. Thorsborne, M., & Vinegrad, D. (2008). The Restorative Justice Pocketbook. Teachers' Pocketbooks.

7. Pranis, K., Stuart, B., & Wedge, M. (2003). Peacemaking Circles: From Crime to Community. Living Justice Press.

8. Amstutz, L. S., & Mullet, J. H. (2005). The Little Book of Restorative Discipline for Schools. Good Books.

9. Braithwaite, J. (2002). Restorative Justice and Responsive Regulation. Oxford University Press.

10. Thorsborne, M., & Vinegrad, D. (2017). Restorative Practices and Bullying: Rethinking Behavior Management. Jessica Kingsley Publishers.

Articles

1. Sherman, L. W., & Strang, H. (2007). Restorative Justice: The Evidence. The Smith Institute.

2. Crawford, A., & Newburn, T. (2003). Restorative Justice and Youth Justice: Bringing Theory and Practice Closer Together in Europe. Willan Publishing.

3. Zehr, H., & Gohar, A. (2003). Restorative Justice: The Concept. Good Books.

4. Hoyle, C., Young, R., & Hill, R. (2002). Victim Satisfaction with Restorative Justice: More Than Simply

Procedural Justice. International Review of Victimology, 9(3), 229-248.

5. Morrison, B. (2007). The Use of Restorative Justice Practices in a School Community. Journal of School Violence, 6(1), 101-114.

Organizations and Online Resources

1. Restorative Justice International (RJI). Retrieved from www.restorativejusticeinternational.com

2. International Institute for Restorative Practices (IIRP). Retrieved from www.iirp.edu

3. Centre for Justice & Reconciliation. Retrieved from www.restorativejustice.org

4. Restorative Justice Council (RJC). Retrieved from www.restorativejustice.org.uk

5. National Association of Community and Restorative Justice (NACRJ). Retrieved from www.nacrj.org

6. Restorative Justice Network of Ireland (RJNI). Retrieved from www.restorativejustice.ie

7. European Forum for Restorative Justice (EFRJ). Retrieved from www.euforumrj.org

8. Centre for Restorative Justice at Simon Fraser University. Retrieved from www.sfu.ca/crj

9. The Little Book of Restorative Justice Series. Good Books.

10. Restorative Justice Clearinghouse (RJC). Retrieved from www.restorativejustice.org

11. IIRP Graduate School's Online Library. Retrieved from www.iirp.edu/library

12. TED Talks on Restorative Justice. Retrieved from www.ted.com

Case Studies and Examples

1. Oakland Unified School District, California. Retrieved from www.ousd.org

2. Restorative Community Conferencing in New Zealand. Retrieved from www.justice.govt.nz

3. Restorative Justice for Oakland Youth (RJOY). Retrieved from www.rjoyoakland.org

4. Community Holistic Circle Healing (CHCH) in Hollow Water First Nation, Canada. Retrieved from www.publicsafety.gc.ca

Additional References

1. McCold, P., & Wachtel, T. (2003). In Pursuit of Paradigm: A Theory of Restorative Justice. Restorative Practices E-Forum.

2. Van Ness, D. W., & Strong, K. H. (2014). Restoring Justice: An Introduction to Restorative Justice. Routledge.

3. Daly, K. (2002). Restorative Justice: The Real Story. Punishment & Society, 4(1), 55-79.

4. Koss, M. P. (2000). Blame, Shame, and Community: Justice Responses to Violence Against Women. American Psychologist, 55(11), 1332-1343.

5. Gavrielides, T. (2007). Restorative Justice Theory and Practice: Addressing the Discrepancy. HEUNI.

This bibliography provides a comprehensive list of sources and references used in this book, offering a wealth of information for further reading and exploration. These resources are invaluable for those interested in deepening their understanding of restorative justice and its applications in various contexts.